Childhood Unlimited

Childhood Unlimited

Parenting Beyond the Gender Bias

VIRGINIA MENDEZ

First published by Sheldon Press in 2022
An imprint of John Murray Press
A division of Hodder & Stoughton Ltd,
An Hachette UK company

2

Sensitivity reader: Georgie Williams

A CIP catalogue record for this title is available from the British Library

Trade Paperback ISBN 9781529395389

eBook ISBN 9781529395396

Typeset by KnowledgeWorks Global Ltd.

Printed and bound in Great Britain by Clays Ltd, Elcograf S.p.A.

John Murray Press policy is to use papers that are natural, renewable and
recyclable products and made from wood grown in sustainable forests.
The logging and manufacturing processes are expected to conform to the
environmental regulations of the country of origin.

John Murray Press
Carmelite House
50 Victoria Embankment
London EC4Y 0DZ

www.sheldonpress.co.uk

To my parents.

To my dad for arguing against me every step of the way, even when he secretly knows that I am right.

To my mum, even if she doesn't want us to get a matching tattoo, for sharing the feminist journey with me and showing me the power of unlearning.

Contents

Foreword ix

About me and about this book xiii

Important note before reading this book xvii

1 Neuroplasticity 1
2 What are stereotypes and what effects do they have? 13
3 Books 30
4 Media: TV shows and films 45
5 Toys 63
6 Clothes 78
7 Language 95
8 Why it matters? Girls 109
9 Why it matters? Boys 126
10 Why it matters? Trans kids 145
11 Now what? 164

References 179

Index 192

Acknowledgements 198

About the author 201

Notes 202

Foreword

by Nic and Cat, founders of the Global Equality Collective

Virginia has given a gift to all parents, and every person working with young people, who wonders how and where to begin with gender equality. *What's the gift?* This book will guide you through the questions you have and the ones you were worried about asking. Virginia is the ultimate mentor – both informing and educating us on what we need to know, and what we didn't previously when it comes to gender equality.

The 'everyday little things' are the driving force behind change when it comes to gender equality. Virginia not only has invited us into her world as a parent of two little humans with *Childhood Unlimited*, but she explores the research and lived experiences behind it too. And, as such, we are invited to sit with her and see the world through her brilliant eyes – and confront the challenges of modern parenting with her.

The little voices of 'stereotypes' are everywhere – they are the ones that tell us what to wear, what to say, where we feel safe to go (and when), what our families think (or should think) and what our line managers accept as 'normal'. But the real shocker comes when, as a parent, you realize that those voices are speaking to kids too – your kids. The systemic biases are present in the aisles of our supermarkets, the advertisements on the TV, and in their nurseries and classrooms.

This book takes that voice, sizes up to it and tells it exactly where it can go.

And that is all due to the author, Virginia. As a member of our Global Equality Collective she is one of our most trusted voices and speakers. Her knowledge and sensitive understanding of all things feminist, activist and fair are second to none. And she is someone we can always call on for a belly laugh.

It is this spirit, drive and expertise that she brings to this book – and into your hands. Her love, passion and evidence-based knowledge make it all so easy and accessible. Virginia also brings together many of our Global Equality Collective members to learn with and from in this book. The result is that in reading this, you will too.

You will be taken on the entire gender equality journey, beginning by understanding why our brains are trying to make life easier with mental shortcuts, but ultimately make barriers and obstacles. You will then review the impact of gender stereotypes on our children, both from Virginia's truths as a parent as well as the research, and plenty of 'takeaways' so you can act too. It will help you create your own bookshelves where you can delight in inclusive, FUN and exciting pages of equality too. Yes, it is possible!

This book will also make you watch TV and films differently, forever. The stereotypes that beam into our homes every day can jar against the messages we teach our students or what they learn at school. As Virginia details, our responsibility is to talk, explain and let our young people review what they think of this – for them to deconstruct the signified meanings and for them to be able to give a distanced reading, a confident and media - literate response to what TV teams tell them they should like.

(Nic) As the mum to boy/girl twins, I know first-hand that the gendering of toys, the choice of clothes they wear and the colours – it is all nonsensical. Toys are a way for children (and adults!) to learn through play. Research tells us that we also learn about identity, role models and stereotypes through the toys we offer to our littlest learners.

This book will teach you why this matters and what you can do next.

When it comes to understanding gender stereotyping on individuals, the research is out there, but listening to Virginia and the incredible lived experiences and voices she has captured in this book brings it all to life. She teaches us that 'normal' is just what you are used to. This book encapsulates everything that we know is the 'norm' for many households out there – and will continue 'to be on the right side of history'.

We read a lot of books on feminism, equality and inclusion, but they can often seem overly worthy, boring and with no call to action. **The opposite is true of this book.**

By reading this, Virginia will also help you to explore the how, the why and the what next with some of the globe's leading DE&I (Diversity, Equality and Inclusion) thinkers and change makers. It will also empower you to investigate and challenge your own attitudes, to shape the experiences of all around you. And YOU will be the one sizing up to that 'voice' in the future, as will your kids too.

Go get them!

We thank you Virginia for bringing to life this incredible library of advice, life and love.

Nic and Cat

www.theGEC.org

About me and about this book

When my father-in-law was reading the beta version of this book to give me feedback, he told me he was surprised that I mentioned that I wanted to change the world with my books:

But I do want to change the world, Malachy.

Do you think you can change the world with your books?

Yes. I do.

You can't say that. That sounds pretentious. Maybe you really will, but you can't say that, definitely not yet.

Of course I can.

So I decided not only to keep that comment in Chapter 5 but also to start the book with it. Because I want to change the world. I want us all to change the world. In fact we all do, every day. It is a matter of how much, or in which direction, but I am a deep believer in collective actions that move things forward. I believe in our power as consumers, as voters, as citizens and, by all means, as parents to change the world.

I believe I change the world when I equip my kids to think openly and to act with kindness. I believe I change the world when I create an ethical company that supports my values. I believe that we all make decisions during our days, from challenging a sexist joke at work to recycling or eating less meat. And all those decisions, in conjunction with a lot of other people's small decisions, have a massive impact.

My story with feminism, like most people's story I imagine, is the story of a journey. From feeling that something was not quite right to starting to understand how deeply wrong it is; it is the journey of unlearning and relearning, of reading lots, having discussions, chewing on them, moving on. I am surprised at my own journey, from refusing to be called feminist to owning TheFeministShop.com. I am amazed at how it has affected every other aspect of my life, from parenting to friendships and career. The biggest thing I have learnt is that once you know, you can't unknow, you can't choose to unsee and you can't choose not to care.

Don't get me wrong, in a way it's a curse. I can tell you that a lot of pleasures have been taken away from me. Simple joys of watching a film with my kids or reading a book are now clouded by anger. Anger that moves me to learn more, to do more, to change things faster.

Don't worry, the purpose of this book is not to turn you into an angry feminist, although I can't promise you that it won't. It is a book about awareness, and data, and tips and tools, so you can make your own decisions and filter what is essential for you and how it fits with the way you want to raise your kids. This book will help you decide what things you are going to limit, which ones to encourage and how to readjust so the things that you pay the extra attention to align with your values. Yours.

I can't tell you how to neutralize a whole society pushing your kids in the direction of being defined by their gender, I wish I could! But I can, and I will, highlight some of the things that perpetuate the message, and give you ideas on how to compensate for it or alleviate it. I will encourage you to put them into practice.

Like I said, I wasn't always a feminist, but by the time my pregnancy test showed me two lines I was definitely one, and I made it my goal in life to make sure my kids, no matter who they were, had as many options and choices to be their true selves. Now, four years later, I have a boy and a girl and have spent an insane number of hours doing research, reading, paying attention, doing workshops with kids in schools, writing books for them, and making sure I know what I am doing, as much as you can be sure of anything at all in parenting.

Becoming a parent also has a very intense way of changing your values and priorities; you become impatient to change things because you are no longer changing them just for you. We want to give our kids all the great things we had in our childhood, while fixing every mistake our parents made, with the best of intentions of course.

It is great to see how parenting is now something we take so extremely seriously, but we need to remind ourselves that we are going to make mistakes, that we are not the only influence our kids have, and trust that they are going to be fine. So let's try our best, let's bring all that knowledge in, the awareness, but also let's assume that parenting, like literally anything else in our life, is a journey we take.

These books will grow with my kids. I will hopefully write another one about their late childhood and pre-teens, and then teenage years, because the challenges will be different and because I can guarantee you that I will keep reading, and researching, and growing with them. I can't predict what society will be like by then, because there's no way of knowing the pace of change, so I am going to focus on the now, on children aged 0–5, and how amazingly important it is to establish good foundations for what is yet to come.

I want this book to be given to grandparents, and to nannies, and to be read in nurseries and pre-schools. I want parents to have something useful and research-based to gift or pass to friends when they are tired of justifying why they do what they do; something to feel like a non-judgemental conversation when they realize that those things matter to them. I want this book to bottle up the thousand conversations I have had with my friends in the last years because I love how they now text me to tell me 'I could almost hear your voice pointing out this or that'. I love it because it wasn't my voice, it was theirs, fully aware and ready to fight it. I want that voice in all of us.

So yes, this is my unapologetic attempt to change the world, or more precisely to prompt you to change it! This is an action - orientated book, one that is written with the goal of you seeing things a bit differently and tweaking things accordingly. I never said that I could fix the world, that would be delusional, but change it? Of course we can. Together.

Important note before reading this book

In order to understand this book, it is important to know the difference between sex and gender. People tend to use both terms interchangeably. But, while connected, the two terms are not equivalent:

- **'sex'** (female/male/intersex) describes biological traits.
- **'gender'** mean personal identity and social construct on how a person lives within society. One's gender identity could be woman, man, non-binary and other possibilities.

Because it is a personal identity and it is socially constructed, gender definitely can't be binary, but according to scientists, neither can sex.[1] When referring to male and female we need to keep in mind that there is a huge variation within those categories, and also big overlaps across them. We are often taught that female bodies have one particular set of organs, hormones and appearances, and that male bodies have another set of organs, hormones and appearances – but the biology is not that simple.

Sex also exists as a spectrum because intersex people exist and can present as a wide variety of biological combinations. Current research estimates that intersex people compose 1.7% of the population,[2] which makes being intersex about as common as having red hair.

While sex is not binary, it is true that sex characteristics tend to be *bimodal*, as Cade Hildreth explains on their website,[3] meaning 'there are *clusters of characteristics* that tend to be associated with people that we call "female" or "male"'.

On average, males do have penises and, on average, females do have vaginas, but it might not be the case with intersex people. On average, males tend to have XY chromosomes and females tend to have XX chromosomes; however, there are at least 16 different naturally occurring variations. Intersex means that a person was born with variations in their sex characteristics. These can include internal genitals, external genitals, gonads, chromosomes, gene expression, hormone levels, receptor sensitivity, brain structure, secondary sex characteristics ...

Gender is even more complex because we have to add a more prevalent factor, individual identity, which is the most important of all. Gender is how we present to the world and how we feel about our individual selves.

This is important in this book because, although I have tried to avoid it as much as possible, sometimes the conversation sounds binary, because that is what society is still used to. Sometimes speaking about something in opposition of something else tends to forget the 'everything' else. I want to make clear that we shouldn't forget it.

It is also important because sex and gender are sometimes considered the same and they are not. Some of the discriminations and realities that a person lives can be directly related with their sex, their biology. Some other times they are the result of their gender. Because this book focuses on the impact that society and its stereotypes play in who our kids become, unless specified directly I am talking about their gender, about the way the children identify and present to the world.

1

Neuroplasticity

It took me what felt like forever to get pregnant. I always knew that I wanted to be a mum and I was at that point of my life where it felt ideal. I had just got married (tick), we both had stable jobs (tick) and I had just moved to another country, so the idea of having a perfect excuse to meet new people and put all my energy into being a mum seemed just great. Every month that I didn't get pregnant added to my frustration. Things were not going according to my plan. I had a clear plan! I was going to be a young(ish) mother of two girls. Period.

I am so thrilled now that things didn't go according to plan. Those were the months that I learnt the most about feminism, the months where a lot of my values shifted and my eyes were opened wider. By the time it finally happened, I knew what mattered and what was going to be really important for me as a mum. I even had a brilliant idea about a book for that kid – a beautiful bilingual children's book against gender stereotypes, to teach them and reassure them that it doesn't matter if you are a boy or a girl as long as you are your true self.

When I thought things were happening the way (I decided) they should, I found out my baby was a boy. I couldn't believe it. And not in a good way. I cried and cried (I like to blame hormones because I feel extremely embarrassed by this). Despite having had a really emotionally draining miscarriage and finally being pregnant with a very much wanted baby, and despite having fallen in love with a book literally about the importance of raising kids free from stereotypes and expectations, I was crying and genuinely sad because I wasn't having a girl.

That wasn't the plan. I was already very proud of how I was going to parent my two (non-existing) daughters. I was going to be the super cool feminist mum who overcame the barriers that society puts on girls. But a boy? A privileged little boy? I felt robbed!

How wrong I was! And how glad I am now that things went that way. Not only because I love Eric and wouldn't change him for the world, but also because it has broadened my horizons and it has become a much bigger and more exciting challenge to parent this way. It is a gift to see the impact on two completely different kids (Nora came 19 months after), and it makes my research more diverse and my interests wider.

The way I raise my kids (avoiding as many biases as possible), the choices I give them and the people they are becoming, does not come free of judgement. People love having an opinion about the way you educate your kids, no matter how hard you try or how long you spend talking about the stereotypes rooted in society and the harmful effects these can have. At some point, normally sooner rather than later, somebody claims 'well, boys and girls just ARE different' and of course they are. It would be impossible not to be when the realities they live are so different from the moment they are born.

That is why this first chapter explores the science behind the nature vs. nurture debate. This is the basis on which we build the rest of the pillars for *Childhood Unlimited*.

Almost everyone is willing to accept that our brains adapt, change and learn. Not only because scientists are in agreement on this point and have shown us the proof, but because it is common sense and we all have experienced it one way or another.

We have all learnt a skill. We have all witnessed children achieving milestones. Some of us have learnt a second language and realize that we understand it without having to translate it anymore. We can drive while talking or singing and just letting our hands and feet do the job, even people like me that failed their driving test six times! We learn to like flavours that we couldn't stand, and songs that we used to love are now only guilty pleasures from the past. Our skills, interests, tastes and capacities change but somehow we think it's rational to assume that girls are born already liking unicorns while boys are naturally predisposed to love dinosaurs.

There have been a lot of experiments regarding neuroplasticity that effectively show how specific events and exposure to different types of learning experiences – such as taxi-driving, juggling or playing Tetris – can change both the structure and function of the human brain.[4] Mindfulness was found to increase cortical thickness in the hippocampus, which is important for learning and memory.[5] Less tangible experiences – for example exposure to social attitudes and expectations – can also change the brain's structure and function.[6]

Even more fascinating, not only has the association between objectively measured socioeconomic status and brain structure been demonstrated,[7] but it has also been shown that perceived socioeconomic status, or where you think you are in the pecking order, can affect brain structure.[8] So not only our reality but also our perceived reality has a massive impact on the way our brain develops; the stories we believe about ourselves can change the neurological pathways of our brain. Just imagine if that story about ourselves is repeated to us over and over and over … the same story repeated by the people we love and listen to, by the TV we watch, by the books we read.

The significance of these findings is that they provide powerful evidence of how 'entangled' our brains are with the world around us.[9] It can take us beyond the old nature vs. nurture debate and illustrate that the way we interact with the world and the way society interacts with us has an effect on our brain and not the other way around. So, by creating completely different experiences for boys and girls from the moment they are born, we are creating a self-fulfilling prophecy – we just like to call it nature.

In a study based on the first whole-brain analyses of 'male/female' characteristics in structures and connections, studying over 1400 brains, it was found that there is no such thing as a 'male' or a 'female' brain. All brains, regardless of the sex of their owner, are a 'mosaic' of different characteristics[10] arising from a range of 'brain altering' experiences.[11] When we specifically look for the differences in our brains based on sex we are missing out the other sources of variability.

If we go into more detail, it has also been shown that many categories of behaviour, cognition, personality and aptitudes that have been assumed to belong mostly to men or to women in reality show very few consistent differences between the sexes.[12] This includes things that are overwhelmingly socially accepted as 'fact', such as empathy being a feminine trait and the assumed natural masculine predisposition to sciences.

This is not exactly new. As early as 1949, Canadian neuropsychologist Donald Hebb introduced the now famous theory that 'neurons that fire together wire together'[13] so, when the connection between neurons is active, their synapses are strengthened and stabilized, while those that are not activated are pruned.

Later experiments confirmed that, via several mechanisms, changes to our brains' neurons are indeed activity-dependent, a feature known as 'synaptic plasticity'. At birth each neuron has thousands of connections; these increase rapidly in the first two years of life until the number of synapses is twice that of an adult brain. Never again in our lives will we have as many synapses as during those first two years.

This is followed by pruning of synapses, which, as Hebb postulated, will be based on use. 'Use it or lose it' and 'use it and grow it'. The brain needs to declutter and the connections that haven't been stimulated enough get discarded.

It is true that we are not born a blank canvas. The brain of a new-born comes with its own genetic predispositions and different defining factors already 'loaded' in from the beginning. But this is 'a starter pack' and our capacity to build on it is the real game changer. When we (consciously or unconsciously) stimulate certain areas, skills and tastes, we are directly affecting the areas which get strengthened or pruned. The early childhood, those first years, is very important for our kids' development. However, we think that they are too small to understand any of the 'important stuff' and instead wait until they are older to have empowering talks. There is so much work that can be done in this early stage, much before the real conversations kick in. We have the opportunity to use their verbal and non-verbal experiences to ensure they don't miss out on developing essential skills.

To break it down, there are indeed differences in the gendered brain, as Professor Gina Rippon, neuroscientist and author of *The Gendered Brain*, explains: 'Our brains reflect the lives we have lived, the attitudes and experiences to which we have been exposed. And if we live in a world where there are many gender stereotypes about what girls and boys, women and men can and can't do, where we are constantly bombarded with gendered messages, those experiences and those messages can change our brains.'[14]

By the time we are adults, men's and women's brains are indeed different. Our skills, our tastes and our inclinations diverge, but we can't simply give all the credit to nature. Rather, these differences have been unconsciously nurtured as well.

The alarming part of this is that much of the time we are not conscious that we are stereotyping our kids. We genuinely believe that we are treating them equally, despite their gender. That lack of awareness about our own biases makes the job of correcting them almost impossible. This is the key part of this book, to bring that awareness and shine a light on things normally ignored, so we can actively correct them and reduce their impact on the early childhood of our kids and all that stems from this crucial phase.

It is important to remember that there is nothing abnormal about being biased. The society we live in is enormously gendered and, because of the self-fulfilling prophecy and dominant narrative, we feel that everything happens in a natural way. We see things around us and believe we have free choices, but do we? It is important to understand that I am not judging the choices in and of themselves and I am not trying to prove that there are good and bad options. It is not about defending blue or pink as the inherently 'good' colour. Instead it is about presenting a whole range of colours so that kids can benefit from what each of them has to offer.

I hear it all the time: 'I haven't done anything, my daughter just likes pink.' And I am sure it is true that she does. I also think there is nothing wrong with liking or doing something perceived as gendered, but we need to understand that the free decisions that we talk about are not as free as we claim them to be. Instead, they have been subtly (in the best cases) pushed upon the child from the moment they were born.

My son's favourite colour is pink, but it is also not a completely free choice. He claimed it as his favourite colour after I dyed my hair pink. I thought it was flattering that he loved pink because he associated with me and I celebrated it, reinforcing his choice. He feels that is our thing. Now Nora's favourite colour is pink. It didn't used to be, but the fact that Eric now always chooses the pink plates or bowls makes her think that there is something special about that colour and she doesn't want to miss out. Of course, these are their choices, and there is nothing harmful about them – I find that colours are morally neutral, they are just colours – but I wouldn't claim that their choice or preference is either innate, natural or coincidental.

Regarding the lack of awareness of our own biases, the BBC did an experiment for their documentary 'No more boys and girls'. The programme studied the way adults deal with gender and kids from a very early stage. They changed the gendered clothes and the names of babies, leaving them with unfamiliar adults to play with them. The differences between how perceived girls and perceived boys were treated was easily spotted. 'Girls' were more often given soft toys and dolls, while 'boys' were physically interacted with more and offered toys that benefit spatial understanding. Differences in the way they were touched, spoken to and entertained were based on their perceived gender.

The documentary also showed those volunteers, reactions when they found out, and of course they were all very surprised and disappointed with themselves. They were shocked because they specifically thought of themselves as open-minded and non-biased. Biases are so ingrained in all of us that they become invisible. The good news is that once you start seeing them, you can't unsee them again.

In the very same experiment, they note how completely different the stimulation is of each of the various toys and how this reinforces different brain abilities. Dolls and role-playing help with empathy and caring skills, while physical play and spatial toys are more useful for sports or science. There is nothing intrinsically good or bad with each of the choices, but it is the lack of awareness, as well as the constant stimulation always in the same direction, that becomes a larger problem down the line. That is why the aim of this book is to dissect some of these biases and make it easier to spot them and correct or neutralize them as easily as possible.

While it can seem disheartening that we are unconsciously enacting our biases, change is possible. I hope this chapter gives you the scientific backup and encouragement we all need to educate our children in a more open way. The following chapters will explore this further and give us the tools we need to do so.

Expert interview: Gina Rippon

Professor Gina Rippon is an international researcher in the field of cognitive neuroscience based at the Aston Brain Centre at Aston University in Birmingham. Her research involves the use of state-of-the-art brain imaging techniques to investigate developmental disorders such as autism. She also investigates the use of neuroscience techniques to explore social processes, including gender stereotyping and stereotype threat.

She is an outspoken critic of 'neurotrash', the populist (mis)use of neuroscience research to (mis)represent our understanding of the brain and, most particularly, to prop up outdated stereotypes.

She is a regular contributor to events such as the British Science Festival, New Scientist Live and the Sceptics in the Pub series. In 2015 she was made an Honorary Fellow of the British Science Association for her contributions to the public communication of science. She is also an advocate for initiatives to help overcome the underrepresentation of women in STEM (Science, Technology, Engineering and Maths) subjects. As part of a European Union Gender Equality Network, she has addressed conferences all over the world. She belongs to WISE and ScienceGrrl and is a member of Robert Peston's Speakers4Schools programme and the Inspiring the Future initiative.

She also speaks on the relevance of contemporary neuroscience to diversity and inclusivity initiatives, and has given keynote addresses to business organizations and government policy groups, including the UK's Cabinet Office.

In 2019, Rippon published her book *The Gendered Brain: The New Neuroscience that Shatters the Myth of the Female Brain*, which investigates the role of life experiences and biology in brain development (published by Bodley Head and Penguin Random House).

Why did you start working on neuroplasticity with a gender optic and why was it important for you?

I focused on this aspect of the story after a meeting of Neurogenderings, an international feminist neuroscience network I belong to. I met up with Cordelia Fine, Rebecca Jordan-Young and Anelis Kaiser and we hatched plans for a paper about the failure of sex/gender neuroscience research to acknowledge the significance of emerging understanding of adult neuroplasticity to theory and practice.[15] So much of the traditional work in this area was based on the notion that biological contributions to brain differences were fixed, inevitable and invariant. Biology was 'destiny' and with respect to the implications of this for an understanding of sex and gender differences and/or gender gaps, it was important that this was challenged. A biological essentialist approach can seriously undermine any attempts at diversity and inclusivity so it was important to draw attention to this.

During your research and journey what was the biggest WOW moment you had, or what was the piece of research that had the biggest impact on you?

An early engagement with such issues was when a review of menstrual cycle research (from a neuroscience perspective) revealed how much self-fulfilling prophecy there is in the 'weaponizing' of female biology. I think the fact that most of the data was collected using a self-report questionnaire called 'The Menstrual *Distress* Questionnaire' says a lot!

Cordelia Fine's *Delusions of Gender* remains a bible in this arena! She and I were working on the same issues in parallel, but she had got her thoughts together much more cogently than me.

Research showing that stereotype threat altered how the brain worked as well as affecting behaviour forms the basis of a core part of my argument about how social attitudes can affect biological processes (and not just the other way round).

In terms of parents as principal educators, if you were to give them two or three practical things that they could start doing right now at home regarding stereotypes in early childhood, what would those be?

- If you can, being a **stern monitor/gatekeeper** with respect to the kind of toy/clothes/stories/media they get exposed to is a good start. You will almost invariably encounter the 'my little girl wants to be a pink princess' and 'my little boy cuts his toast into the shape of a gun' phenomena, but being aware of the source of this and how many influences even tiny children are exposed to can be eye-opening.
- **Call it out!** Where you (or your children) do encounter sexist stereotypes, find a way of challenging them (if, say, in their school environment) and/or having a conversation with your children about them. 'Do you think only boys can be super-heroes?' 'Can only girls do ballet?' 'Why do girls have to have all the pink stuff?!' etc. Complain if your school Christmas fair is heavily gendered (Lucky Dip for boys, Lucky Dip for girls) or if the pictures of famous scientists are all male.
- Find as many **counter-stereotypical** examples as you can: wonderful feminist fairy stories such as The Paper Bag Princess, or books about boys wearing dresses or becoming ballet dancers or nurses. See <http://www.lettoysbetoys.org.uk/category/gift-guides/> and <https://www.notonlypinkandblue.com/> for suggestions.

For those parents wishing to learn more, are there any particular websites, books, videos, podcasts or other resources you would recommend to help them?

The Fawcett Society has recently published a report on the effect of gender stereotyping in the early years, packed with examples and recommendations about stereotyping in parenting, education and the commercial sector: <https://www.fawcettsociety.org.uk/the-commission-on-gender-stereotypes-in-early-childhood>. This is a brilliant, wide-ranging resource (and not just because I was involved!).

Education specific: Lifting Limits <https://www.liftinglimits.org.uk/> is focused on schools but has lots of information and resources for anyone concerned with stereotyping in early education. The Fatherhood Institute <http://www.fatherhoodinstitute.org/> helps fill the many gaps in advice for men, as does Men in the Early Years <https://miteyuk.org/>.

Toys, books, clothes: Websites/grassroots campaigns such as Let Toys Be Toys are brilliant: <https://www.lettoysbetoys.org.uk/about/>. Also look at books such as *Cinderella Ate My Daughter* by Peggy Orenstein and *The Gender Agenda: A first-hand account of how girls and boys are treated differently* by Ros Ball and James Millar.

If you take away just a few key points from this chapter, let them be these

1 Scientific research proves that brains have a huge capacity to change: we are not born with tastes, capacities and abilities set in stone.
2 The first years of life are very important in terms of brain development. What we stimulate will get stronger, what we ignore will weaken.
3 What we consider free natural choices for kids evolve from a mix of everything they have experienced from the moment they are born.
4 Biases are deeply ingrained in society and we all have them. Once we are aware of them, we can start to correct them.

What to do next

This chapter only requires a bit of introspection. Take just five minutes to allow yourself to ask questions and try to go further.

- What things do you love? Do you remember when you started loving them? What kind of memories are associated with them? Would those life experiences have been the same if you were a different gender?
- What things do you dislike, or feel that you are bad at? Do you remember when you started loathing them? What kind of memories are associated with them? Would those life experiences have been the same if you were a different gender?
- What stereotypical skills, attitudes, tastes do you have? How have they been reinforced because of your gender?
- What counter-stereotypical skills, attitudes, tastes do you have? Where do they come from? How did your gender interact with it all?

2

What are stereotypes and what effects do they have?

Eric and Nora are not very aware of gender, but they are extremely aware of genitalia and refer to their body parts with insistence and curiosity. They also ask about everybody else's parts, especially in public and especially with people we don't necessarily know! For two tiny humans so interested in vulvas and penises, I don't think they have any idea yet of the expectations that most people associate with them – which, if we think about it, even for a minute, is a very weird concept.

Because I am Spanish and our language is very gendered, I quite often find myself in the position of explaining why I use a masculine word instead of a feminine word, and somehow having to link it back to their genitalia as I can't find another reason to explain why it is cow and bull, cock and hen or why Nora is my daughter and not my son, for example.

Being, as I am, really aware of the importance of creating a space for kids to explore their gender in an open way rather than through strict standards, I don't feel particularly comfortable with any of this. If either of mine happens to be transgender I would like to know that they have always had room to openly speak, ask questions and feel loved and welcome. But for now, when they ask, I am forced back to the information that I think they will understand best. 'Well, you know how mum and Nora have vulvas? That's because we are girls and girls are daughters and not sons' and vice versa. I could go through the whole gender and sex difference, but considering they are only two and four years old, it feels a bit much, so I just add a 'it is a bit more complicated than that, but we will talk about it sometime in the future'.

Eric loves playing superheroes and houses, pretending to own a shop, to go to a spa, running, reading and doing shows. He likes painting his nails, jumping in puddles, scooters, bikes, baby dolls and cuddles on the sofa. He is not afraid of kissing or saying I love you and is, overall, a sweet, sensitive child. Since he was two I have been asked if I am worried about him being gay, or if I am concerned about him choosing 'girly' things. The truth is that he doesn't solely choose those things that are normally understood as for girls (not that I believe that there are things for boys or for girls to start with), he chooses a huge variety of things, most of them completely overlooked when they meet traditional gender expectations (like playing Lego), but the ones that are slightly unexpected create unwarranted concern. The unexpected choices (and I am talking completely natural things like him pushing a pram or dressing up as Elsa) add up and they generate unease to the point that people feel they have to address it with us as parents, that feeling of *it* being a thing that we can't pretend is not there. Here's my typical response:

> 'No, I am not worried that Eric is gay. First of all because I don't find homosexuality worrying, but also because he is a very small kid and I don't think he has yet any romantic or sexual interest for his own gender or any gender in particular, which is what homosexuality is about.'

That question highlights the stereotypes and phobias we, as a society, have, and how they affect a child's upbringing. The fact that people confuse gender with sexuality, how we link behaviours and preferences with gender and, really worryingly, the fact that we think sexual orientation is something that parents can, and should, correct.

Whatever gender my kids happen to be, and whatever their sexual preferences, my role is not to limit them or decide their ways but to support them and help them navigate any obstacles. This most likely means first having to unlearn things myself.

At this moment in time, both Eric and Nora seem completely fine with who they are and how they are perceived. They are completely unaware that their vulva or their penis comes with baggage and that people will treat them differently because of it. They find their sex to be something fun to touch, sing songs about, sometimes even choreograph, and proudly parade naked around the house, despite the cold. That's all. And I am happy about it.

My kids are extremely different from each other and neither of them conforms to their narrow gender moulds (show me a child that does!), yet I often get praised for Nora's toughness but worried looks about Eric liking sparkly things. I mean, *it sparkles!* How can I explain to him that fun things like sequins and glitter are not meant for him *unless he is gay*? That he needs to prefer grey joggers over glittery, colourful outfits because, and only because, *he has a penis*?

Why? Because of stereotypes.

Stereotypes can be useful. We use them to make sense of the world because they reflect general expectations about members of particular social groups and they help us determine what information we need to remember or value. They are a useful filter through which we process objective information. Considering we receive an insane amount of information every day, stereotypes make the job of processing that information easier and faster. But of course, they come with downsides.

Gender is one of the first features we identify in people and this gives any associated stereotyping an even bigger impact. We implicitly group unknown individuals by their gender, even when this category doesn't add any relevant information to the situation. We say, 'I spoke with a woman' instead of 'I spoke with a person' even if the fact that the person was a woman adds nothing to the conversation or context. Our brain has learnt that it is an important category and we frequently reinforce this idea, even if unconsciously.

Additionally, even though there is enough evidence to prove otherwise, we continue to define gender as binary, comparing men and women and highlighting the differences between them. 'There are only two, opposing genders' feels much easier to navigate than accepting a spectrum in which individuality has to be celebrated. But this traditional way of doing things, even if apparently easier, has not only proven to be incomplete and flawed, but also very damaging.

Gender stereotypes, like any other stereotypes, exaggerate and oversimplify reality. By doing so, they reinforce beliefs and justify the social differences. It is much easier to accept the inequality when we think it responds to a natural predisposition, rather than accepting the role society has in it and, in a way, the role we have in it.

Trusting that we are very different, and that those differences justify the different outcomes, shocking statistics or experiences, liberates us from the idea of having to do something to change it. Gender stereotypes are shared by everyone regardless of their gender – we are all users or perpetrators and targets or recipients of them, and it is going to take a global effort to change the narrative.

We have already seen in the previous chapter how different experiences shape who we become. Stereotypes are the rules that define and narrow those different experiences. Stereotypes are the presumptions that the world holds about us and they limit everyone because they take hold from an extremely early age, suppressing many of the characteristics that make us ourselves.

For example, there is a lot of research-based evidence that shows gender-stereotypical expectations influence the way we judge the abilities, among other things, of women and men. Naomi Ellemers reviews this extensively as part of her *Annual Review of Psychology* about gender stereotypes.[16] That means that all of us, regardless of our gender, tend to perceive the same objective performance differently depending on the gender of the individual performing it. Think not only about the repercussions at school, but also about parents perceiving the capacities of their own kids (and further down the line enhancing and promoting them). In a study from 2014, aggregate data from Google searches showed that of all Google searches starting 'Is my 2-year-old', the most common next word was 'gifted'. But this question is not asked equally about young boys and young girls. Parents were two and a half times more likely to ask, 'Is my son gifted?' than 'Is my daughter gifted?'. Parents show a similar bias when using other phrases related to intelligence that they may shy away from saying aloud, like, 'Is my son a genius?' On the other hand, parents Googled 'Is my daughter overweight?' roughly twice as frequently as they Googled 'Is my son overweight?'.[17]

A good example of this unconscious bias is via one of the broadly accepted 'truths' (a.k.a. nothing more than gender stereotyping) that female students are less talented than male students in all areas of science. I know that for some this might seem like an old belief, but the research published in 2019 by the UK Department for Education still finds very different attitudes towards STEM subjects depending on gender already by the age of 13/14.[18]

The way bias works makes it possible to maintain that outdated but persistent belief even if studies, like the one carried out by the University of Colorado, document that women are outperforming men in both physical and life science courses. Men continue to be perceived as equal or better students.[19] And that is possible because even when we are presented with data such as the above (that debunks our previous beliefs), we are less likely to take it in because we're already conditioned to think the opposite. It has been documented quite extensively that when processing information, we tend to consider the observations that match our stereotypical expectations as more plausible than the counter-stereotypical ones.[20]

This illusory correlation, a false association between two variables, ties in with the 'assimilation' theory proposed by Jean Piaget.[21] Assimilation maintains the status quo as we perceive the world in ways that make it fit our existing beliefs, sometimes reinterpreting these new experiences so that we don't need to change previously existing assumptions but just add on top of them. Accommodation, on the other hand, is when old ideas are changed or even replaced based on new information. For example, in our unconscious efforts to maintain those comfortable presumptions, we misremember the information from our own experience in a way that confirms our stereotypical ideas. An experiment in France showed the correlation between people who held strong (stereotyped) beliefs and the way they remembered their own grades. Girls who believed that women were worse at maths than men remembered their own maths grades as worse than they really were, while boys holding the same stereotypes remembered theirs as higher than the ones they actually got.[22]

Furthermore, when the successes or failures in performance match what our internalized biases expect, we believe that they are reflecting individual talents and abilities. On the contrary, when they don't match those expectations, we unconsciously attribute this to external circumstances (such as help from others) or temporary conditions (for example, an easy assignment, exceptional effort or cheating). A study carried out with third and fourth grade teachers[23] considered strong test results from boys in their class as indicative of their natural ability for logical reasoning, whereas the identical achievements of girls were attributed to exceptional effort. When the boys' performance was low, it was perceived as lack of effort, but in the case of the girls, the results were considered indicative of a lack of ability in logical reasoning. I am giving examples from teachers and classrooms because they are quantifiable. But what about our own expectations with our children? How do we unconsciously understand and support their development based on what we think are their talents and abilities?

If we look at mathematics, two different studies from 2018[24] found no gender differences in basic numerical skills in infants and children. Another study[25] does show very small differences in maths performance, with boys doing slightly better, at high school and college age (but that may be attributable to acquired skills rather than natural ones). Either way, even if we look at the studies that found the largest gender differences, in terms of mathematical performance boys and girls are much more similar than they are different. Decades of research, in a meta-analysis that included 242 studies from 1990 to 2007,[26] show that there is not really a clear factual difference in *performance*, as it is still believed.

What's really interesting is that despite the lack of real difference in *aptitudes*, there is a visible effect of stereotypes on *attitudes* to maths. Girls have higher levels of maths anxiety and lower levels of confidence in their maths skills, with anxiety already negatively linked to maths performance in girls as early as 8 years old.[27] This means that even when girls show similar performance levels to boys, they are often less sure of themselves. It seems clear that this is the natural result of living in a society that sets clear expectations through stereotyping and dissuades girls from building that confidence. To me this is so key: the real differences lie in *attitudes*, not aptitudes. And unfortunately, those attitudes come from the world in which we live. It is also positive in a way as we can change that, we can help our kids to make the most of their aptitudes, no matter what they are, by equipping them with the right tools to manage the attitudes.

This whole unconscious protection of stereotypes is what causes us, despite the evidence, to keep coming back to the fact that we are different, and we keep justifying it under the premise that it is nature. We do so because we need to feel that the world operates as a meritocracy and that we are the sole designers of our destiny. We want to believe in meritocracy so much that we avoid seeking or even accepting evidence that proves that our success is often aided by different privileges, opportunities, the way we are perceived and the way the world treats us.

This happens with all sorts of stereotypes, from class to race. As long as we claim that the different life outcomes, preferences and societal roles are nothing but individual choices, including our own, we can maintain the idea that we have equal opportunities, and it is all a matter of free will. A study of stay-at-home mothers indeed established that those who believed their situation was the result of individual choice were less inclined to recognize workplace barriers and discrimination as a source of gender inequality.[28] There are a lot of reasons for any parent to choose to stay at home, from financial to willingness to spend more time with the kids, from social pressure to logistic reasons, and those personal reasons can coexist with the realities of gender equality at work, inequalities that push women to be the main ones making that move. However, we need to believe that we make our own choices, and that differences in society are nothing but the result of a lot of informed and free choices made by individuals.

In general, and this applies to every protected group, the belief that social differences come from individual choices allows us to ignore the fact that members of different groups are not treated equally, and if we ignore this, we don't have to do anything to fix it. By convincing ourselves that women freely choose the roles that society gives them, we're excused from having to change things.

It is easier to believe that women just happen to prefer to be the secretaries of the bosses than the bosses themselves, that they choose to dedicate more time to household chores than their partners do when in heterosexual relationships, that they prefer to always be the main caregivers at the expense of their careers, that they willingly carry the family mental load. If those are choices, and they are natural choices as women are naturally better at those roles, then there is nothing wrong with it, and we can keep operating as usual.

Believing that there is a direct relationship between individual merit and societal outcomes protects people from guilt about their privilege. That is why those who benefit from these differences are often the first to downplay and deny the group-based difference in the first place. For example, men are much more reluctant to accept the validity of empirical evidence showing the role played by gender stereotypes in the underrepresentation of women in STEM fields, especially men that work in these fields themselves.[29] There is something rather ironic about scientists refusing to trust scientifically proven correlations because it just hurts their illusion of meritocracy and calls into question how much of their own brilliance got them where they are! I get it, it is uncomfortable to see the ways in which our experiences have been easier than for others, it is natural to hold on to the value of our effort or skills. But this is not about what you had to do; it is about what someone else (black, woman, with a disability …) would have to do to get the same outcome.

The truth is that it is a vicious circle. Gender stereotypes reflect gendered roles in society, and they are difficult to alter because we don't see enough different people in different roles, but, of course, that is complicated to change because stereotypes make those transformations so challenging. As complicated as it is, I think this is the best place to start, educating ourselves as parents and carers so kids can get things better from the beginning, becoming, proactively and on purpose, the role models that they need and their cheerleaders and supporters to break the moulds.

So yes, it starts by doing the work on ourselves. It can feel a bit daunting to recognize that part of who we have become, what we like or what we do, is due to societal expectations. But it can also be quite liberating to understand that certain things we are holding on to are only the result of stereotypes and the expectations that come with them. As parents it is easier to do the job for our kids than for ourselves, and I love that determination, but I would highly encourage you, while you are reading more about this topic, to 're-parent' yourself a bit, and allow yourself to ask further questions. Sometimes that will come with the grief of feeling that we could have done more, or better, if we had been given the chance; other times it will come with the discomfort of understanding our own privileges (if not because of gender maybe because of race, or body ability, for example). I know it is not fun, but it is very difficult to create an open space for our kids if we are not allowing the same for ourselves.

The first step is to accept that we are all subject to gendered expectations and that these may bias our judgements of our kids, the same way that our parents and the world were (unconsciously) biased about us when we were children. Accepting that society as a whole is rooted in these generalized beliefs makes it possible to identify and correct such biases and allow a less stereotypical and restricted life experience for the new generations. While we can't control everything for them, it is a great start to teach them to think critically, and to challenge those stereotypes as part of their routine. We can only do that if we take on that exercise ourselves as well.

This chapter has some daunting and serious points to make, showing as it does how stereotypes are so deeply ingrained in society that our brains work naturally to preserve them – so much so that we may even trick our perceptions of a situation, our memories, and even question the data rather than change our ideas. Unlearning what we have learnt is more complicated than we think.

But, let's finish on a high point. Since we now know how deeply accepted those stereotypes have become, and how we are all affected by them, we will be even more ready to stay alert and readjust our natural instinct to defend our bias. It is the power of awareness that gives us the advantage. We've got this, we understand now the complexity and impact of stereotypes. We also know that no matter how much we get it, it is still super-ingrained, and it just isn't possible to get it right all the time. It is liberating, knowing that we can be wrong, understanding why and being open to change. It is a journey. We can stop being defensive and focus on moving ahead and applying strategies to avoid passing this burden on to small children and, most importantly, allow them to naturally develop with all the benefits of a broader and more neutral context.

Expert interview: Christia Spears Brown

Christia Spears Brown, Ph.D., is the Lester and Helen Milich Professor of Children at Risk in the Department of Psychology, and founding Director of the Center for Equality and Social Justice, at the University of Kentucky (previously at UCLA). She earned her Ph.D. in psychology at the University of Texas at Austin. Her research focuses on children's perceptions of gender and ethnic discrimination, the development of stereotypes and group identity, and the impact of discrimination and stereotypes on children's development. In addition to more than 75 peer-reviewed journal articles and book chapters, she has written four books, two for academic audiences, *Gender in Childhood* and *Discrimination in Childhood and Adolescence*, and one for parents, *Parenting Beyond Pink and Blue: How to Raise Children Free of Gender Stereotypes*. Her newest book, *Unraveling Bias: How Prejudice Has Shaped Children for Generations and Why It Is Time to Break the Cycle*, focuses on how race, immigration, gender and LGBTQ bias is embedded in our laws and policies, and how children are affected by those biases. She is an Associate Editor of the *British Journal of Developmental Psychology*. She is a Fellow of the Association of

Psychological Science and was the Society for Research in Child Development Scholar-in-Residence. She regularly speaks and consults with parent groups, schools, toy and media companies, and professional organizations about reducing the impact of stereotypes, is regularly featured in national media outlets, and has served as an expert witness for the American Civil Liberties Union on cases of gender discrimination in schools.

Why did you start working on the effects of gender stereotypes on kids and why was it important for you?

I actually began graduate school to study the effects of stereotypes, both gender and race stereotypes, on children's development. My graduate advisor at the University of Texas at Austin, Rebecca Bigler, was doing some of the best research on this topic and that is why I went to work with her. I always thought knowing the effects of gender stereotypes was important because gender stereotypes are so pervasive. Before graduate school, in the mid-90s, I was at a McDonald's ordering a Happy Meal for a child I was nannying and the cashier asked if I wanted a boy toy or a girl toy. It struck me how much weight we place on simply knowing someone's gender to make all sorts of assumptions about what they would like to play with. It was my lightbulb moment. After that, it was easy to notice how much we pay attention to kids' gender in every domain of life – it is the first question a pregnant mother is asked, toys are colour-coded, specific activities are chosen, friends are segregated based on gender. And that doesn't even begin to address all the restrictions placed on people because of their gender. I remember being told 'boys don't make passes at girls who wear glasses' and being told to sit 'ladylike'. I think those are outdated concepts now, but it is still obvious that our culture's obsession with gender categories affects how kids grow up. So I went to graduate school to study exactly what was going on and how children were affected.

During your research and journey as an expert what was the biggest WOW moment you had, or what was the piece of research that had the biggest impact on you?

The research that had the biggest effect on me was done by my advisor, Rebecca Bigler. She went to an elementary school and randomly assigned half of the teachers to 'use gender' in a functional and meaningful way. They sorted the classroom into girls and boys, they referred to the class as 'Good morning, boys and girls', they had a pink bulletin board and a blue bulletin board, they would ask the class 'to line up, boy, girl, boy, girl'. Pretty much everything a typical class does. There were no gender restrictions or stereotypes (no one said 'Boys are so strong' or 'girls are so sweet'), they just used gender to sort, organize and label the children. The other half of the teachers were asked to never use gender, to just refer to children as individuals or find creative ways to sort and organize that were not gender-based. Bigler found that after six weeks of these classrooms, children in the gender classroom endorsed stronger gender stereotypes than children in the control classrooms. Just using gender as a meaningful grouping led children to lean into gender as an important category and develop biases about gender. We since replicated that study using fake groups based on red shirts and blue shirts. Just like with gender, kids would create and believe stereotypes about these colour groups when the teacher said, 'Good morning red and blue group' and 'Let's line up red, blue, red, blue'. This taught me that it wasn't about gender per se, it was about how our society *uses* gender as a meaningful way to organize people.

In terms of parents as principal educators, if you were to give them two or three practical things that they could start doing right now at home about gender stereotypes and kids, what would those be?

- The first is to **stop using gender as a label**, colour code and way to talk about people unless it is really relevant. This means thinking about how we label people ('there's a man on the street' could be 'there's a person on the street'), how we talk to our kids (instead of saying 'what a smart girl you are' say 'you are so smart' or 'what a smart kid'). Make gender a less prominent part of how we think and talk about people. Otherwise, children notice that gender is *the single most important* characteristic of a person.

- The second is to **point out stereotypes you notice**. Help children to learn to spot them. Also, point out when gender is used in ways that are irrelevant. This can mean pointing out how crazy it is to have an aisle of toys labelled boy toys and an aisle of toys labelled girl toys. Make every time you notice gender a teachable moment. It is important for parents to know that most children believe gender stereotypes, even the children of very progressive parents. Unless parents are actively talking about gender stereotypes, children will absorb the stereotypes out there and even make up their own (my own daughter once told me that only boys like oysters because she, as a girl, did not like oysters). Helping kids learn to spot stereotypes and label them as stereotypes means that even when they encounter stereotypes in the future, they will be more immune to them.

- The third is to **correct every gender stereotype you hear kids or adults say, even the silly ones.** When an adult says 'you know how boys are' or 'girls are so helpful' in earshot of your child, talk to your child afterwards about that as a gender stereotype. When your child says something about gender, talk to them about it. We want to prevent children from the either/or thinking inherent in stereotypes (*either* girls like this *or* boys like this).

For those parents wishing to learn more, are there any particular websites, books, videos, podcasts or other resources you would recommend to help them?

I, of course, recommend my own book, *Parenting Beyond Pink or Blue*. I also highly recommend *Pink Brain, Blue Brain* by Lise Eliot to learn about what actual gender differences are and are not.

I think the A Mighty Girl website (<www.amightygirl.com/>) is a really good resource for children's books. <Genderspectrum. org> has a lot of resources about gender and gender identity. Learning For Justice (used to be Teaching Tolerance) has great classroom resources and discussion starters about gender stereotypes that can be easily adapted by parents. <Mediasmarts.ca> in Canada has some great information about talking to kids about how men and women are portrayed in the media.

I also recommend the videos Miss Representation (about biases facing girls <https://www.youtube.com/watch?v=W2UZZV3xU6Q>) and The Mask You Live In (about biases facing boys <https://www. youtube.com/watch?v=hc45-ptHMxo>).

If you take away just a few key points from this chapter, let them be these

1 There is overwhelming evidence showing that we attach expectations and perceived ability to gender – almost always unconsciously.
2 The brain naturally accepts observations that align with stereo-types, whereas it puts counter-stereotypical outcomes down to external circumstances or temporary conditions.
3 The illusion of meritocracy perpetuates gender stereotypes, ignoring privilege and systemic gender inequality.
4 As parents we should first examine and challenge our own pre-conceptions, motivations and expectations. We don't need to be harsh on ourselves for having them, it's normal, but we need to unlearn a lot of what we have learnt.
5 Because of the way stereotypes work and how difficult it is to completely avoid them, it is really important to aim for progression and not perfection. It is a journey!

What to do next

- Think about a stereotype the existence of which you believe is normal, something that you believe is different between boys and girls and that everyone has accepted because it is true. Now try to understand how you came to believe it. When was the first time you assumed it was true? Do you remember the first time you heard about it? Did you ever challenge or just accept it? Do you realize and reinforce it when you see it happening? Have you ever seen counter-stereotypical cases? What do you normally think when you see those 'exceptions'? How has society reinforced this stereotype (media, books, jokes ...)? Have you reinforced that idea yourself when speaking with others? Have you researched it to understand where it comes from or just assumed it a fact? Go as deep as you want asking yourself questions about your relationship with the stereotype. Obviously, we cannot do that with everything (who has the time?!) and a lot of the stereotypical thoughts and beliefs that we hold are unconscious ... but we can start having an idea on how *we* work with stereotypes and challenge them when they become limiting beliefs. A couple of examples to get you started ...
  - Men are more simple
  - Women are worse drivers
  - Girls are more emotional
  - Boys don't like dolls
- Try journalling about gender stereotypes that you spot during the day. Try to keep a notepad on your phone or do it as an exercise in a notebook at the end of the day (there's some space to take notes at the end of this book). Maybe aim to do it just for a week, or for a month as an awareness exercise. (I suggest this activity for kids, and it works wonders!) Every time you are able to spot a difference in the way you or your kids are treated based on gender (when you see it in an advert,

or in a casual conversation ...), make a note. You don't have to have big feelings about it or think it's very important, and you don't have to morally judge it or the person behind it. You can just notice that there is a difference based on gender and make a note of it. Start 'collecting' them – you will have a pretty decent variety very soon.

3

Books

So, there I was, finally pregnant and growing more feminist by the day. I was definitely a bit scared about everything that was to come, but to be honest I was mostly excited, full of hormones and pumped to do my part to change the world. I had just got my positive pregnancy test, so that meant I had about 8 months to dismantle the patriarchy. Spoiler alert: it didn't happen.

I have always wanted to be a writer since I fell in love with books and realized the amazing power of words to transmit a message. So it just made sense to me to make both my childhood dreams come true. Becoming a mother AND a writer; and not just any writer, but one that my kids would be proud of. If I couldn't manage to change the whole world at least maybe I could change theirs.

That was the beginning of it all, what would become my first children's book. I had an idea of writing the perfect book for my bilingual baby and then I realized that if that book was perfect for my child, it would be perfect for many other children.

When I got into a creative mood, I made some notes of things I felt were essential to include in the concept of the book:

- Narrated by a girl, hearing her voice, seeing the world through her eyes.
- Two characters, a boy and a girl, both completely relatable to any kid and both defying some of their gender expectations.
- Curious, happy kids. Kids that both parents and children would like.
- Positive role models: bodies that are kids' bodies, clothes that are kids' clothes, attitudes that are appropriate for their age.

- A father very involved in their feminist upbringing. The father as a key figure in education, being emotional, accessible and responsible. Stop only representing mothers as main carers.
- Two main goals: invite and educate on critical thinking and reinforce self-esteem. We are all different, we are all unique and special.

I understood, while writing it, that there was a lot of power in giving the kids the opportunity to educate adults too. On some topics, like gender stereotypes, adults tend to become defensive when speaking with other adults. Children's natural curiosity and questioning of ingrained realities can bring some context to the absurdity of a lot of these things. How do you explain to a kid that it is normal to treat people differently? How do you say that the same tears, the same hug, can be bad for one child but not for another? Kids don't judge in the same way adults do – using this approach gives freedom to the adult to apply the same critical thinking that otherwise might have been ignored without further thought.

That is as far as I got while pregnant: just falling in love with the idea and starting to write notes. I finished the story in London, in a cafeteria, while breastfeeding Eric. Chris took a picture and said, 'We will remember this moment forever' and he was right. Four months later I was pregnant again.

During my second pregnancy I contacted illustrators, did the last edits, translated it and finally, as I waited in the hospital to deliver Nora by c-section, I sent the email with the definitive version to the publisher so they could start printing it. It took six weeks for the book to arrive, and for my c-section scar to heal. My life, once again, had changed dramatically and that first book, *Mika & Lolo*, about two cousins on a journey to defy gender stereotypes, was in my hands.

When I decided to write the book, I didn't know just how necessary it was. I just knew it was a great tool to educate on something that had become my biggest passion. I was excited about what I could do with it. Since then, I have read and researched a lot, and I have experienced first-hand the horrors that we let our kids consume. My passion for children's books aligned with values has only increased.

There are two main studies focusing on children's books:

1. *Gender & Society* made a study of nearly 6,000 books published from 1900 to 2000[30]

First thing worth noting is that this study is over 20 years old now, and thankfully things have changed lots, but to be honest most of the change has happened in the last years, and it is very important to understand that they have changed because the market – the public – has demanded this change.

There are signs that books with a more forward-thinking approach are selling through, parents are tired of the same old stereotypes. Remember, publishing houses will always follow the money – it's worth noting that we vote with our pockets, and that we, the consumers, are agents of change.

Anyway, this study made some fascinating discoveries:

1 Males are central characters in 57 per cent of children's books published per year, while only 31 per cent have female central characters.
2 No more than 33 per cent of children's books published in any given year contain central characters that are adult women or female animals, but adult men and/or male animals appear in all of them.
3 Male animals are central characters in more than 23 per cent of books per year, while female animals are in only 7.5 per cent.
4 On average, 36.5 per cent of books in each year studied include a male in the title, compared with 17.5 per cent that include a female.

5   Although books published in the 1990s came close to parity
    for human characters (with a ratio of 0.9:1 for child characters;
    1.2:1 for adult characters), a significant disparity of nearly 2 to
    1 remains for male animal characters versus female.

In their deeper analysis they noted that since children's books
are a *'dominant blueprint of shared cultural values, meanings and
expectations'*, the disparity between male and female characters
is sending children a message that *'women and girls occupy a less
important role in society than men or boys'*.

Kids love books. Books help them understand the world
and open them up to completely different realities. But books
also send messages, not necessarily consciously, about what is
expected of women and men, and they shape the way children
will think about their own place in the world.

In seeking to answer why there is such persistent inequality
among animal characters in books for kids, the authors say
some publishers – under pressure to release books that are more
gender balanced – use *'animal characters in an attempt to avoid the
problem of gender representation'*. However, their findings show that
most animal characters are gendered and that inequality among
animals is greater, not less, than among humans. On top of this,
there is a clear tendency of readers to interpret gender-neutral
animal characters as male, which exaggerates the pattern of female
underrepresentation. Two different studies note that mothers
show, when reading books, extreme masculine bias, almost always
labelling gender-neutral animal characters as male when reading
with their children.[31] Other studies show that children naturally
assign gender to gender-neutral animal characters.

What I found really interesting is that the youngest children,
4 to 5 years old, usually assigned their own gender to the
characters. The 7 to 8-year-old and 10 to 11-year-old children
were influenced by gender stereotypes, assigning animals gender
based on their role in the story (e.g. solitary bears were less likely

to receive female labels).[32] As the authors of the study claim, *'animal characters (...) could be particularly powerful, and potentially overlooked, conduits for gendered messages... The persistent pattern of disparity among animal characters may reveal a subtle kind of symbolic annihilation of women disguised through animal imagery.'*[33]

Given that I am a mother and I have to read an insane number of children's books, after reading this study I became really careful to ensure that I avoid that symbolic annihilation that is now ingrained in my brain. By default, whenever I read any books, I usually swap a few things around and try to make the very large majority, if not all, characters female and I specifically try to gender characters as male when that gives an opportunity to defy stereotypes (so mostly for teachers and parents). I know it sounds extreme, but if everyone else in my children's lives reads those books normally (their grandparents, at school, the occasional friend that wants to humour them, their uncles and aunts) I feel that overcompensating on my side is probably still falling short in the grand scheme of what we are fighting against. Also, the fact that my decision to make all of them female can cause more discomfort than the fact that the original texts often contain only men, perfectly highlights the strange and twisted situation in which we find ourselves.

Sometimes I change the gender of a character, previously read by someone else, and Eric corrects me. 'No mum! It is a boy!' I love it when that happens, because I can ask why. He then tries to justify the answer with the picture ... and it normally ends up with an honest 'I don't know' and he buys into the new name and personality. Chris then gets corrected afterwards when he goes back to the original: 'No dad! It is a girl.' A lot of the time what kids long for is constant repetition, security in what is happening. Stereotypes can provide that comfort. Knowing that the short-haired farmer is a man and the person with the skirt is a woman gives them a sense of control and understanding, those are labels that they have been exposed to long enough to assume that they are correct. That is why it is important to open up those labels and boxes at this stage, when they are honest and respond, 'I don't know' and they happily engage in a challenging conversation.

Normally, after having agreed with Eric and Nora about the new name and gender of the characters, I run a quick game in which I ask them three or four questions along the lines of 'Who is [insert stereotypical item] for?'. I normally take this quite seriously, put on my show voice and pretend we are in a televised contest. So if it was long hair that made them decide that it was a girl, or the fact that it was a dinosaur made them think it was a boy, I start there. 'Who is long hair for?' (fake microphone in hand) *EVERYONE*! 'Who can like dinosaurs?' *EVERYONE*! It doesn't take long and it anchors once again the reassurance that everything is for everyone. We're all people. There really is only one big and important label and we all fit in.

As I said at the beginning, the aim of this book is not to convince you to do what I do, but rather to raise awareness and enable you to decide which of these things are important for you ... and what you want to do about them. To me the word 'annihilation' did wonders in making me take a step back and think. It's such a powerful word that it almost felt like a symbolic genocide. Now, it's the happy face of my kids when they are celebrated for getting all the answers right in our personal show that drives me forward.

Another, more recent study, is not dissimilar.

2. *The Observer* 100 most popular children's picture books of 2017

In this research, an in-depth analysis of the 100 best-selling children's book of 2017 (including favourites like *The Gruffalo*, *Guess How Much I Love You* and *Dear Zoo*), the conclusions are not any more promising:

1   Male characters are twice as likely to take leading roles in children's picture books and are given far more speaking parts than females.
2   Female characters are missing from a fifth of the books ranked.
3   Male villains were eight times more likely to appear compared with female villains. Only one book, *Peppa and her Golden Boots*, portrayed a sole female villain, acting alone: a duck who steals Peppa Pig's boots and takes them to the moon.
4   There were three male characters present in each story for every two females featured.

Women adults undertaking caring roles were common in the stories. For example, it was twice as likely for a teacher to be a woman than a man, mothers were also present almost twice as often as fathers, and fathers rarely appeared alone. As the researchers state, '*This reflects a skewed version of the world which is bad for boys as well as girls. The lack of fathers, for instance, steers them away from an interest in nurturing and caring behaviour.*'

It is not a coincidence, nor is it just nature, that girls are more driven to careers and life choices in caregiving. Instead, we learn to identify ourselves as part of a group and gender seems to be the group that is easiest to divide into, one that comes with very repetitive rules and role models. In order to fit in we just need to follow those rules and copy the role models. Being mothers and teachers is how girls see themselves represented in books. Then, because it's a self-fulfilling prophecy, they of course also usually have their mum as their main caregiver and their primary school teachers are statistically more likely to be women too. Unless we are proactively promoting other options, unless they see themselves in other facets and they see other people taking over the joys and burdens of providing care, it is no surprise that girls believe that motherhood and teaching are the natural paths for women, if not their natural fate.

The same goes for the boys: the fact that they are not exposed to male role models undertaking caregiving tasks stops them from thinking that those tasks or roles apply to them. If they never see a man teacher in any of the media they are exposed to, in the main caregiver in books and, according to statistics, at home, how can they build up a narrative of a world in which everything is for everyone? In which all the career options are for everyone, and co-responsibility at home is the basis of everything else?

This is not only about the cost to the individual but also the cost to society due to the misallocation of talent that closes off fruitful career avenues to both girls and boys. We are missing out on excellent men primary school teachers and great women making decisions at venture capital businesses. But it is not only the words in stories that are problematic; studies of children's literature that have focused on illustrations have all found biased or stereotypical visual representations of gender.

One study was carried out looking at image representation of gender in children's science books in public libraries.[34] It found that images of males as scientists were used three times more often than images of female scientists. *'The women were generally depicted as passive, lower status and unskilled – or their presence was not acknowledged at all.'*

Another study shows how female characters in children's books are often shown in lower status jobs, such as secretaries rather than bosses, and males are more often pictured as adults or superheroes.[35] Even the positions they show in the illustrations follow the same stereotypes and messaging, with more women in sitting positions that appeared more submissive than the male characters, and women literally taking up less space than men.[36]

All this is important because stereotypes in illustrations *'significantly affect gender development'* and provide children with *'a stockpile of images for children's mental museums'*.[37] There is a parallel story happening in the images and it's a story packed with a heavy load of subtle messages that reiterate what kids are seeing and hearing everywhere else.

I don't think illustrators, publishers and writers consciously or in a harmful, twisted way want to indoctrinate our daughters into submission from early stages via this subliminal messaging. If only it were that easy! The problem is that our bias and understanding of the world are present in the way we do things and we unconsciously spread them unless we are aware, and actively correcting it. I am confident that those illustrators, publishers and writers would be surprised to know not only that they have been spreading this message, but also how it contributes to a bigger problem. I have a lot of hope for the world, I genuinely think that most people want to do things better but are simply unaware of what they need to change, and each and every one of us is on a learning journey. I know that because it happens to me, all the time.

I am genuinely proud of my book, *Mika & Lolo*, but someone told me once that it would be great to have more diversity in the race of the characters. They specifically said, 'We loved it, but my kids always ask, at the end of each book, why there are not more kids like them and it would be great if they could see themselves in the next one', and it almost made me cry. Because it is true! I didn't consciously make a white family to erase the BIPOC (black, indigenous and people of colour) community, I just didn't think any further than what was closer to me, than what was my normal. Replicating the narrative that we are used to, with the same genders taking the same stereotypical roles, is not mal-intentioned, but instead what we are used to from years and years of blind spots, and it's the default or easy way to tell our stories. Don't worry, Mika and Lolo made racially diverse friends in the second book, which is all about consent. That is what changing and introducing diversity means for me, not about feeling guilty or making those changes a chore but realizing it and using that new knowledge to act differently.

Just because books and reading, in themselves, are positive things for kids, and just because most children's books try to address important issues (caring about nature, being brave, being kind, etc.), it doesn't mean that they are not participating in the stereotypical education we give to our kids. Books deeply shape our children's understanding of the world so it is essential that we ensure the things that we read to them are helping them to see the world in a more open, diverse and inclusive way.

The great news is that children's books options are vast, and growing, and there are already lots of gems ready to be the next favourite in your house. We can, and we should, aim for both a good message AND different gender role models, and we shouldn't have to compromise.

Expert interview: Jayneen and Jess Sanders

Mother and daughter, writers and passionate about gender equality

Jayneen Sanders is an experienced early years educator, author, publisher and blogger. She writes children's books on body safety, consent, gender equality, respectful relationships and social and emotional intelligence and has written over 130 children's readers. She believes empowering children from an early age makes for empowered teenagers and adults. Her ongoing passion for the safety and empowerment of children continues today with new manuscripts and free-to-download resources always in the wings. You can find her work at <www.e2epublishing.info>.

Jessica Sanders is an author and social worker; however she considers herself as more of a 'social impact entrepreneur'. Jess has a passion for creating resources that nurture positive mental health and promote gender equality. Every project she pursues is born from the question, 'Why does it have to be this way?' Jess's first book, *Love Your Body*, is the perfect example of this. The book, which was originally crowd-funded through Kickstarter, was born from Jess's refusal to accept that every girl is destined to grow up disliking her body. Not only is negative body image a waste of a girl's precious energy and time, it also holds her back from achieving her full potential. Jess has since published *Me Time*, a self-care guide to be your own best friend, and the follow up to *Love Your Body* for boys, *Be Your Own Man*. Jess spends her day writing books, facilitating school-based workshops and drinking ridiculous amounts of coffee.

Why was using books for kids as a way to pass on important messages important for you?

Jayneen: As an early years educator, I have always used books to impart important messages to children. Children are such visual learners, so picture books are the ideal medium to pass on crucial learnings. Picture books evoke discussions around social and emotional learning such as empathy, compassion and feelings and emotions. They can also impart messages around consent and gender equality. Hence why books were the obvious choice for me to pass on the learning I know kids need. Also, I have always been a storyteller, so combining my skills in this area with key messages for children was the perfect partnership.

Jess: I'm really passionate about ensuring that children receive positive, inclusive and protective education at a foundational level. As adults we have all had to unlearn harmful messages or seek out knowledge and insights that were missing from our own childhoods. This takes time, labour and privilege. It's so much easier to learn things correctly from the ground up and that's why getting in early is key.

What was the biggest WOW moment you had regarding the importance of children's books or what was the thing that stuck with you about the importance of gender diversity in children's books?

Jayneen: The biggest WOW moment was in a school library session with 5 and 6-year-olds. I was looking for a book to read to the children about pirates. But ALL the books within the library featured only male pirates and I thought OMG! This is ridiculous! So, I decided to write a book right there and then about a female pirate. I also realized that most stories of action were led by boys and being an adventurous child and woman, also being married to a male feminist where we brought up our three daughters equally, I thought things need to change. And they need to change from the very beginning – literally as soon as a woman knows she is pregnant. Children are read books from the very beginning of their lives and what is in them greatly influences their view on the world. So, we MUST have a gender - equal and diverse representation in our children's literature.

Jess: When I heard the line, 'children cannot be what they cannot see', that kind of made everything become clear for me. I think about this idea in every book I create.

In terms of parents as principal educators, if you were to give them two or three practical things that they could start doing right now at home regarding the books they buy, they read, they choose – what would those be?

Jayneen:

- Choose books with diverse and gender-equal characters.
- Change the 'voice' around in books, e.g. make the butterfly the male character and the bear the female character.
- Purchase alternative fairy tales, in particular where the girl rescues herself and is the lead in her own adventure. And if you do read more traditional fairy tales, unpack them and use them for discussion on gender stereotyping.

Jess:

- Make sure that gender, ability and body diversity are included. You'll notice that most books have a male protagonist. Try integrating more books with female protagonists.
- Pick books that build emotional intelligence and literacy. Empathy and emotional intelligence are incredible tools

to support a child throughout their life and you can start teaching them about these things early.

- Find books that align directly with their interests or introduce them to new ideas. Again, children can't be what they can't see – so supporting them to learn about lots of different professions, activities and people allows them to dream big.

For those parents wishing to learn more, are there any particular websites, books, videos, podcasts or other resources you would recommend to help them?

Jayneen: A Mighty Girl on Facebook, Instagram: Level Playground, Woman of Impact, 1 Million Woman, Lunarbaboon, geccollect, gecrebels, thinkorblue, educate2empower, jayneensanders-author.

Jess: A Mighty Girl, Mamas Together: Community & Nervous System Regulation, Level Playground.

If you take away just a few key points from this chapter, let them be these

1 Studies conclude that female characters, female animals and male carers/teachers are underrepresented in kids' books. Illustrations also play a big part in the same message.
2 Even gender-neutral animals in kids' books tend to be interpreted and read as male by parents. Kids apply genders to non-gendered animals based on stereotypes. Non-gendered caring figures are interpreted as female.
3 Children's books are key tools in development and a disparity between male and female characters impacts how children perceive their importance and their role within society.
4 We don't have to compromise. We can encourage kids to read while also using books as a tool to show them diversity and counter stereotypes.
5 As buyers we have a say. The ever-growing demand for socially conscious books is driven by the also ever-growing demand as consumers of children's books aligned with our values in a rounded way. Let's keep pushing in that direction.

What to do next

- There is a fairly straightforward test that I use when choosing books to buy for children. There are three things that I check:
  - **Illustrations**: Are the genders simplified and overly represented (big eyelashes, colour coding in their clothes, stereotyped features/outfits/hobbies, etc.)?
  - **Story line**: Are there boys and girls (male/female animals, etc.) and are they all active characters? Are those characters repeating the stereotypical narrative?
  - **Lesson**: Think about how the kids are going to feel after the book. Are they going to identify with the characters and are those characters positive role models?
- Take a book that you already have in the house and try to change the gender of all characters when reading it. See how you feel about it. If it is awkward ask yourself why. If your kids are old enough, this is a great thing to do with them and make it part of a bigger conversation. What do they spot that is odd? Why is it strange? Why do they think that matters?
- If there are books that directly go against the kind of role models, messaging or ideas that you want, just give them away. Fewer but better books, especially when children tend to enjoy the same books over and over, is great.

If you don't know where to start, this is a list of 25 really good books for kids that are about diversity, strong role models and good values. And they are fun!

Remember that this is for both boys and girls. Boys need to read about women and it is really positive that they normalize them as role models as well. (List is in alphabetical order.)

1 A *Big Bright Feelings* book by Tom Percival (collection)
2 *A Is for Activist* by Innosanto Nagara

3 *And Tango Makes Three* by Justin Richardson and Peter Parnell

4 *Doctor Li and the Crown-wearing Virus* by Francesca Cavallo

5 *Fastest Woman on Earth* by Francesca Cavallo

6 *Good Night Stories for Rebel Girls* by Elena Favilli

7 *I am a Warrior Goddess* by Jennifer Adams

8 *I Like Myself!* by Karen Beaumont

9 *I look up to Malala Yousafzai* by Anna Membrino and Fatti Burke

10 *Julian is a Mermaid* by Jessica Love

11 *Little People Big Dreams* collection (various authors)

12 *Love Makes a Family* by Sophie Beer

13 *Mary Wears What She Wants* by Keith Negley

14 *Morris Micklewhite and the Tangerine Dress* by Christine Baldacchino

15 *My Body, What I Say Goes!* by Jayneen Sanders

16 *My Family, Your Family!* by Kathryn Cole

17 *My First Book of Feminism (for boys)* by Julie Merberg

18 *No Means No!* by Jayneen Sanders

19 *One Love* by Cedella Marley

20 *She Persisted Around the World* by Chelsea Clinton

21 *Sparkle Boy* by Leslea Newman

22 *The Boy with Big, Big Feelings* by Britney Winn Lee

23 *The Colour Monster* by Anna Llenas

24 *The Fog* by Kyo Maclear

25 *The Paper Bag Princess* by Robert Munsch

4

Media: TV shows and films

I don't know about you, but I definitely thought I would let my kids watch less TV than they actually watch. I still think we're doing ok (using the technique of comparing yourself with the national average or the friend that is worse than you) but it's definitely not the life of wooden toys and creative activities that I envisioned before realizing how hard being a parent actually is. TV is the most similar tool that I have found to a pause button, and I refuse to judge or be judged for needing one.

I genuinely believe that they actually might get more educational material from a good TV show than from me at 6 a.m., when I am useless and grumpy. The problem is which programmes to choose, because children's brains are massive sponges and things that they see and hear, no matter how subtle, do help to compose their idea of reality.

Children's TV shows are one of the things that really upset me a lot. I am just letting you know in advance, because once you open this door there is no way back. You will start to question and notice how the same patterns repeat over, and over, and over.

As with the books, we find that most shows are genuinely trying to teach some good values: love for nature, teamworking, bravery … it is just that they keep doing it in an extremely stereotyped way – with little to no diversity, causing more harm than good. Also, because the things that all those shows have in common are those stereotypical structures, they are the things that keep being reinforced.

CBeebies would be our default, it avoids the HORROR of the adverts aimed at kids and, in general, they make an effort to present shows that are somehow educational. Yet, in a weekday morning, most of the shows are male dominated (*Justin's House, Mr Tumble, Timmy Time, Bing, Hey Duggee, Go Jetters, Peter Rabbit, Octonauts*). It is only after two hours that you get 11 minutes of a female lead in *Bitz and Bob*.

It is not just one show, it is one after another, after another. And children (and adults) assume that it is ok that females don't get to be the leaders unless the shows cater specifically for girls in a very obvious and stereotyped way (pink, sparkles, unicorns, etc.).

It is time to demand a more guilt-free pause button, to be able to let our kids learn from other mediums without undoing the hard work done at home while we are half-asleep on the sofa or trying to get the very many other things done that need our attention.

There is a great term, coined in 1991, called 'The Smurfette principle': a group of male buddies will be accented by a lone female, stereotypically defined. Boys are the norm, girls the variation; boys are central, girls peripheral; boys are individuals, girls are typified. Boys define the group, its story and its code of values. Girls exist only in relation to boys. It is 30 years old now but sadly stays as fresh as if it were new. Think of *Paw Patrol*, to mention a very current and very popular series (which, in fairness, recently had to incorporate new puppies in response to the critics). We have the clumsy, the brave, the kind … and the girl! Whose whole personality is, indeed, being a girl. Being a girl in a lot of shows, still now, is a whole personality.

Can you think of a TV show or film for kids with 50/50 girls' presence (or, god forbid, even a majority) that is not marketed as a programme for girls? And let's go a bit further, how does society feel when boys like those films and shows and use them as role models?

Society has tricked us to think that a male lead is mainstream, and a female lead is niche, even if we are over 50 per cent of the population. And this beautiful trick starts in the very early stages ...

For example, children love *Frozen* (and Disney love it even more because it has been a money-making phenomenon). I, too, love a lot of things about the film. I obviously think there is a lot of work to do in some of its other aspects (from diversity, to encouraging a healthier body representation of what is considered beautiful) but, in general, it has a lot of great things and, controversially, I find Olaf hilarious. And, of course, kids like *Frozen* too. It is a story about friendship and family; it is magical, has a great soundtrack, loving characters ... naturally boys would love to be Elsa as much as girls. She has superpowers! And children are obsessed with superpowers. Why shouldn't they want to be like Elsa? Why are boys discouraged from using an Elsa backpack? Why can we find thousands of items tailored for girls with the face of Elsa on them, including pants, but not for boys? If I want a Spider-Man outfit for Nora, I can easily find a 'sexy' (why? she's 2 years old) girl's Spider-Man dress or I can safely put her in a boy's costume, knowing she won't be judged or laughed at.

Why are most women proud to share that they were such tomboys, but you don't find men bragging about having been very 'girly'? Why do we have that natural rejection with men admiring and exploring feminine figures, but we are comfortable with girls watching TV shows and media that either under-represent or severely stereotype them?

I deliberately chose *Frozen* because it's actually a rare example of a film that provides feminine role models that boys are willing to embrace, even if society keeps trying to stop them from doing so. I guess a lot of people consider *Frozen* one of the big examples of how the narrative is evolving into an egalitarian one. And it is. But did you know that in *Frozen* most of the lines (59 per cent, to be precise) are spoken by male characters? Think about it (if you haven't watched the film yet you might have a bit of homework to do): apart from Anna, Elsa and their mother, pretty much every other character is male. Kristoff, Olaf, Sven, Hans, Oaken, Pebbles the head of the trolls, the dignitaries that come to the party, the kingdom advisors … as much as I celebrate the changes, it is undeniable that Arendelle is still pretty much a men's world.

But don't trust me and my now obsessive realization of how wrong visual media for kids is, let's go and see what experts say. There are two main organizations that are leading the research: Common Sense Media, and The Geena Davis Institute on Gender in Media. Both analyse how gender representation stacks up in visual media, as well as the effect this can have on children and society. I can't recommend enough that you join their newsletter and be up to date with all the amazing work they are doing to change things.

The Common Sense Media report was published in 2017 following a thorough analysis of more than 150 academic journal articles and numerous press articles. Please read the whole report as it is fascinating and very detailed but, as a quick summary, and for the focus of this book, the most relevant conclusions are:[38]

1 Media reinforces the idea that masculine traits and behaviours are more valued than feminine traits and behaviours

You might think it would take many years of exposure for those ideas to take an effect, but the research shows that the more a 4-year-old watches TV, the more likely they are to believe that the world sees boys and men as better than girls and women. Better. 4-year-olds. Let's stay with that thought for a minute.

Also, to make it a bit scarier, the idea of what those masculine traits look like includes aggression, power, dominance, status-seeking, emotional restraint, heterosexuality, and risk taking.[39] If I think about my own son, I know those are not things that naturally exist within him, but I have no doubt that he will nurture them if they are presented to him as the traits he should display, and traits that are the most highly valued.

2 Media promotes the notion that girls should be concerned about their appearance

There is evidence that exposure to appearance-focused TV content increases body dissatisfaction among 5- to 8-year-old girls[40] and has an impact regarding self-objectification (viewing oneself as an object whose external appearance matters more than internal qualities),[41] which is associated with many negative outcomes, including diminished academic performance,[42] decreased body esteem, increased anxiety, decreased confidence in maths ability,[43] body shame and depressive symptoms.[44]

So, by exposing them to appearance-focused TV (also known as most of TV!) we are opening them up to an increase in body dissatisfaction. It is just not possible to live to those unrealistic standards and it can be highly demoralising when it is repeated that appearance is one of our higher (if not the highest) values as girls and women.

3 Heavier viewing of gender-traditional television content is associated with children's gender-typed career aspirations as well as holding stricter ideas around chores.

Girls who consume more traditional TV programmes express more interest in certain, traditional careers for women.[45] Girls who are shown TV clips that feature women with stereotypical behaviours express less interest in STEM than girls who are shown no content or who are shown clips featuring female scientists.[46] Some of those experiments are done with short TV clips, but what happens when that same messaging is replicated in many shows, in many books, in the way kids are spoken to, the way their clothes send a message? Kids are sponges and they are learning about the world and themselves with the information around them.

What I found most fascinating about this whole piece of research was the explanation of why the impact on children is so big – it is because the stereotyping is adequate to their level of understanding.

The programmes aimed at very small kids have very obvious differences between genders: long vs. short hair, lengthened eyelashes vs. not, dresses vs. trousers, pink vs. anything else, etc. Because of the cognitive immaturity of kids the differences are more rigid and obvious. Basically, it is 'stereotyping for dummies', just in case kids miss the fact that we are very different and that those differences are important. Making sure that kids clearly differentiate both groups makes it inevitable that they also start getting tips about the different behaviours, roles, outcomes ... and those, too, tend to be stereotyped.

Once children start growing and understanding and their personal experiences expand, they discard some of the rigid differences, and so does the media tailored for them, but still they maintain the ones adapted to their level; older kids are capable of accepting more nuance, but the segregation increases. Media starts catering for boys and for girls in a segregated way, reinforcing again the idea that gender is a very important difference, and those segregated programmes are filled with stereotypes adapted to their cognitive stage: desired behaviours, occupations, interests, etc. We have now the programmes for boys (more violent), the programmes for girls (about socializing, beauty and caring) and the ones for everyone (which of course have mostly boys/male animals as main characters).

The process continues until adulthood (where it remains strong), following them in their milestones: beauty standards, romantic aspirations, work, chores, sexuality ... The huge power of stereotypes in TV during childhood is how media adapts them to cater for their cognitive situation, modifying them and readapting them to fit every new stage. More refined and subtle ones exist further down the line, but still always strongly supporting the differences that we insist on calling 'nature'.

The other big researcher is The Geena Davis Institute on Gender in Média. As one of the many things they do to change the narrative of diversity and inclusion in the media, they present an annual report that analyses the representations of gender, race, LGBTQ+ identity, disability, age and body size in popular children's TV shows.

The last one, carried out in 2020 analysing programmes aired in 2019, found the following key points when analysing TV shows for gender (I recommend you read the whole report to see the other very important and interesting categories):[47]

- 45 per cent of children's television episodes have a female lead, a decrease from 52 per cent in 2018.
- Female characters account for a majority of screen time (58.7 per cent) and speaking time (58.8 per cent) in live-action kids' TV shows, which is higher than any previous year we have studied.
- Compared with male characters, female characters are three times more likely to be shown in revealing clothing or partially nude.
- Male characters are more likely to be shown as violent and twice as likely to be depicted as criminal than female characters.
- Male characters are more likely to be shown in professional positions such as doctors and lawyers, while female characters are more likely to be shown in service positions.
- Among characters in STEM professions, male characters outnumber female characters two-to-one.
- Two-thirds of children's TV episodes pass the Bechdel-Wallace Test.

In case you don't know what the Bechdel-Wallace Test is, it was devised in 1985 by cartoonist Alison Bechdel and her friend Liz Wallace. They use three simple questions to evaluate if a film includes a positive representation of female characters:

- at least two women are featured;
- these women talk to each other;
- they discuss something other than a man.

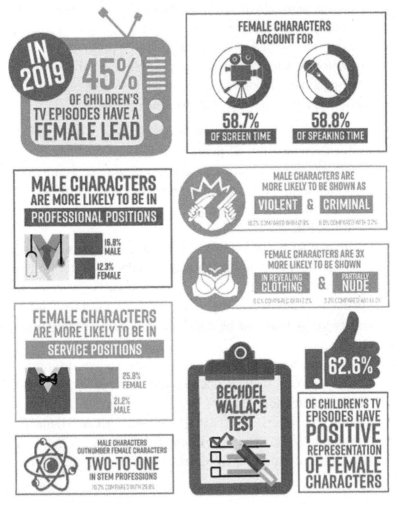

Infographic by Geena Davis Institute on Gender in Media – shared with permission

When analysing family films, the results show that:[48]

- We have achieved another historic milestone: for the first time, lead female characters have reached parity in the top-100 grossing family films! The percentage of female leads in family films has doubled from 2007 (24 per cent) to 2019 (48 per cent).
- We see signs of progress with female characters' speaking time in family films. The percentage of speaking time has increased from 31.3 per cent in 2014 to just under 40 per cent in 2019.
- The percentage of female characters' screen time has also increased nearly 10 points since 2014 – from 34.9 per cent to 42.6 per cent in 2019.
- When it comes to female leading characters, 67.3 per cent are white women and 32.6 per cent are women of colour with a huge underrepresentation.
- We have not seen much progress with gender and supporting characters. Male supporting characters still outnumber female supporting characters two-to-one.
- Female characters are six times more likely than male characters to be shown in revealing clothing.
- With age, a majority of female characters in family films are under age 40, while a majority of male characters are age 40+.

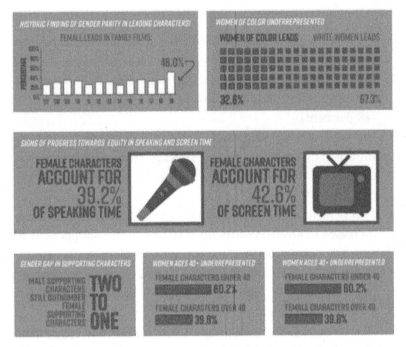

Infographic by Geena Davis Institute on Gender in Media – shared with permission

In a joint project with Promundo focusing on masculinity under the title 'If he can see it, will he be it?'[49] they studied gender stereotyping in kids' media, using the most popular children's shows aimed at kids from 7 to 13. Because that age group is not the main target of the book I don't want to go too deeply into the findings (although I recommend you read it), but to sum up: TV still shows male characters committing most of the violent acts, being less involved in hands-on parental duties, but of course engaging more in risky activities, to name just a few.

There is a third really interesting study by Hopster carried out in 2019[50] that analysed the different stereotypes in shows aimed at pre-schoolers (observing 50 most popular shows for kids age 3–4). I like that they examined the representation of different protected groups (race, disability, class, gender, LGBTQ ...)

and made further observations about the negative stereotypes regarding single mums or fat people. For the aim of the book I will focus only on the gender ones:

- Some of the most positive, popular and long running shows still feature unhealthy gender stereotypes, e.g. males as the knowledge bearers and protectors, and women who clean.
- In many cases, male protagonists are shown to be more powerful or important than their female counterparts, taking on the roles of doctors or policemen.
- In the most extreme examples, female characters were shown being undermined by males.
- Looking further into female stereotypes, a considerable amount of objectification was noted in the 50 shows examined.
- When it comes to males, as well as having overly muscular physiques, males were typically the troublemakers within storylines (or the villains).

It is so very positive that those aspects are starting to get measured and reported and that we can objectively understand that, when we demand better, the industry is forced to do better. We have a say on what gets produced, and we make a statement every time we choose *Postman Pat* over *Dora the Explorer*, or *Paw Patrol* over *Bitz and Bob*. The industry just wants to sell, and by consuming products that match our values and stopping viewing the ones that go against them, we are taking a more powerful stance than we think, and we are also making sure that our kids are getting a more diverse idea of the world.

The good thing is that it has also been proven that benefits accrue when watching counter-stereotyped TV. It is linked to more interest in traditionally 'male' careers among girls and more flexibility about housework for both genders. Furthermore, and you might be as shocked as me by this, what the studies consider 'counter-stereotyped' is simply what I would describe as normal – desirable normality if you will – but definitely not something weird or alienating: *'strong and capable female characters who are not obsessed with their appearance and with attracting males, who initiate and lead, and who enjoy outdoor activities, sports, science, and technology; and male characters who collaborate with girls, respect them as equals, demonstrate empathy and emotions, and resolve conflict in nonaggressive ways.'*[51]

There are programmes like that, and these are the ones that we should be choosing. If we do this, we can actually use TV as a positive reinforcement of what we want to present as normal in our household. But yes, let's of course not forget our pre-parenting goals of wooden toys, arts and crafts and outdoors play!

Expert interview: Melanie Hoyes

Mel can often be found consuming, musing, analysing and discussing film and popular culture. Having completed postgraduate studies and teaching film and TV at undergraduate level, the British Film Institute (BFI) has given Mel the opportunity to use these skills in a contemporary industry context. She completed a BFI research project to historically map ethnic diversity in onscreen representation in UK film for the Black Star season at the BFI Southbank in 2016, ground-breaking research and data methodology which she continues to speak about to a variety of audiences. The research was also written up in a piece in *Sight & Sound* magazine and an academic collection of essays called 'Black Film, British Cinema II'. In her role as Industry Inclusion Executive, Mel advocates for increased access and equity in the UK film sector as well as consulting and partnering with global partners to embed diversity and inclusion into policy and practice. In particular, Mel champions the BFI's Diversity Standards and seeks to establish data and research as a baseline for meaningful change. She is also the Europe Council Lead for The Geena Davis Institute on Gender in Media.

Why did you start working on the media industry and the impact of different stereotypes and why was it important for you?

As a mixed race, British woman, I feel like I am trying to locate myself every day. I am continually trying to establish what being an intersection of all of those identities means to me and how that places me in the world and country I live in. Doing so in the books, film and television I love to consume feels like a natural fit. Initially this took the form of consumption for pleasure, moved into studying and focusing on representation in film and media, and eventually led to working in the film industry, attempting to bring light to these issues and essentially trying to change things.

There is immense power in images and the ability of film and TV to influence people's hearts and minds, and how they view the world, cannot be underestimated. If all audiences see are negative tropes and one-dimensional portrayals of humanity, the way in which they experience and interact with the world can be blinkered. It's hugely important to me to try to move the dial in order that future generations are able to see every version of themselves onscreen and imagine and realize the potential contained in their unlimited, multifaceted and nuanced stories.

During your journey and your experience on the ground, what was the biggest WOW moment you had, or what was the piece of research that had the biggest impact on you?

My academic background and the work I have undertaken in diversity data and research have solidified my status as an information nerd! I truly believe in the ability of data and research to draw focus on the issues we face in terms of representation and inclusion in the industry, whilst holding our progress, or lack of it, to account. The pioneers of this work in the industry are mainly Hollywood based – The Annenberg Inclusion Initiative, The Hollywood Diversity Report and The

Geena Davis Institute on Gender in Media all paved the way in terms of regular reporting on the actual status of representation on and offscreen and threw into stark relief what we knew to be true anecdotally. In 2017, the BFI did a deep dive into the gender stories contained in our database of UK feature films, the BFI Filmography. There were many insights from this longitudinal research into the participation of women in the industry but there was one that resonated with me that I still refer to today. There is an assumption that, in terms of representation and diversity, we are always progressing and things are improving. However, this research showed that this simply isn't the case. Onscreen and offscreen representation of women in UK feature films averages at around 33 per cent since 1911. There have been peaks and troughs in this time but the average remains the same, proving the need to consistently work towards providing opportunities for women in film and media. This statistic is always on my mind in my job and embedded into my practice as I try not to perpetuate this stagnant statistic and am driven to make meaningful and long-term change.

In terms of parents as principal educators, if you were to give them two or three practical things that they could start doing right now at home about their media choices and how to approach the impact they have, what would they be?

The key to thinking inclusively is to continually interrogate your choices and practices. Children learn so much from the media, images and stories they consume, so there's an incredible impact to be made just by making sure those narratives and representations are as varied and diverse as possible. If all of the protagonists your children are exposed to are white, able-bodied, cis-male, heterosexual, etc. they will inevitably have a narrow view of who gets to be a hero/succeed/exist comfortably in the world.

We are incredibly lucky in the UK as children's television is some of the most diverse and representative content there is, but this can easily extend to film, games and literature too. If you're not seeing the diversity you'd like, put in some time to research authors and creators you should invest your time and money in – the internet is abundant with all sorts of lists of representative material. Ensure that the narratives are not perpetuating damaging or limiting stereotypes (e.g. Disney princesses reliant on a male saviour) or at least be aware of when they exist and question them. Highlight complex and nuanced representations as positive and to be celebrated.

For those parents wishing to learn more, are there any particular websites, books, videos, podcasts or other resources you would recommend to help them?

- The Geena Davis Institute on Gender in Media's research is so enlightening on this subject and has several research papers about the representation of women through an intersectional lens.[52]
- There is a lovely short film and article that rounds up the main points around the importance of representation and has a comprehensive list of references to expand your reading on the subject – *The Importance of Representation in Film and Media* by Lauren Wash ington.[53]
- *Girls on Film* is a podcast by film critic Anna Smith which reviews films from a feminist perspective. Episode 79 discusses the evolution of the Disney princess and gives some good recommendations for newer films that challenge and subvert this stereotype.[54]

If you take away just a few key points from this chapter, let them be these

1 Media makes us believe that boys are mainstream and girls are niche. It feeds the idea that masculine is neutral and feminine a variation of the default.

2 There is a big resistance to letting boys have female role models, which is an important part of the problem.

3 Stereotypes are adapted, in the media, to the development states of the children, with more obvious and rigid ones in the beginning and more subtle ones as they mature.

4 Because the stereotypes are adapted to their life milestones, accentuating the difference of the groups within that particular life stage, they have a bigger impact in how they perceive the world, themselves and what is normal.

5 There are data and reports available that not only help us do better but also serve as a benchmark for the industry to step up. Awareness is proven to be a gamechanger.

What to do next

Remember that we have a choice regarding what our kids watch, especially nowadays when a lot of things are on demand. I recommend you watch something (even briefly) before giving them the choice to watch it.

- The most famous test, in order to spot sexism in a film, is the Bechdel-Wallace test. But we can ask ourselves some questions when watching TV with the kids to understand how we feel about the impact it is having:
  - **Character appearance**: Do the way the characters look send messages about the importance of looks in a disproportionate way for girls? Are the body shapes healthy? Is their clothing very stereotyped? Are their body shapes sexualized?
  - **Story line**: Do both boys and girls feature (or male/female animals) and are they all active characters? Is everyone

having positive adventures? Are those characters falling into a much-repeated narrative?

- ○ **Lesson:** How are the kids going to feel after the programme? Are they going to be empowered to be better? Are they going to have better self-esteem? Are they going to identify with the characters and are those characters the role models they should be?

- If you are watching something with your kids and they are old enough to have simple conversations, bring up the stereotypes that you spot, use them to have a talk to point out why that is not ok. What do you think about the way the mum is always cleaning and cooking and serving? In our house who does it? Who do you think should do it? Why? Just see what they are thinking, what is sticking and where you think you are going to push a bit more or bring more conversations to reinforce the critical thinking.

- If there are shows that directly go against the kind of role models, messaging or ideas that you want to give, just explain to them that you don't want them to watch them because you don't like the way they represent girls/boys. You can explain that there are many good TV shows and no need to watch something that doesn't respect what we believe in. It is good, from very early stages, that they find that sexism, racism, homophobia, etc. are off limits in our choices.

If you don't know where to start, this is a list of 20 really good shows for kids

(List is in alphabetical order)

1 Bluey
2 Charlie and Lola
3 DC Super Hero Girls
4 Dino Dana
5 Doc McStuffins

6 Dora the Explorer
7 Hilda
8 Jojo & GranGran
9 Lili's Driftwood Bay
10 Luna Petunia
11 Maisey
12 Masha & the Bear
13 Molly of Denali
14 My Little Pony
15 Peg and Cat
16 Puffin Rock
17 Sarah and Duck
18 Sesame Street
19 Stella and Sam
20 Steven Universe

5

Toys

I think one of the biggest clichés of aspirational parenting is wooden toys. That promise you make yourself that your kids will only play with beautiful wooden toys, that in your house there will only be super educational games and quality things. You're going to go back to good and simple.

Chris and I were convinced that we wouldn't buy plastic or toys with noises, and to be completely fair we haven't done it much … but we also haven't bought many of the good ones. We are, as my mum judgementally calls us, 'cheap parents'. I like to say that we are environmentally conscious, but to be fair it's probably a mix of both. The toys in our house are gifts, or hand-me-downs from generous friends and neighbours and some charity shop treasures. And there is definitely a fair share of noisy plastic in the house (some of those do, of course, get 'accidentally' given away or lost in transit). All this is just to say that I am not judging anyone, I know that there is usually a huge difference between what we *expect* to do and what we actually end up doing.

The good thing is that kids love to play with anything. They love the expensive toys and fake laptops, but one could argue that they like the cardboard boxes from parcels and the random household items even more: the bottle opener, plastic bottles, Tupperware, clips, pegs and any kind of stationery, kitchen tools, make-up brushes, etc. Whatever kids get their hands on automatically becomes a toy, and if you have more than one child then that latest 'toy' immediately becomes the absolute favourite and most desired toy of all! Kids have a huge capacity to invent toys to fulfil their natural demand for playing, discovering the world.

I remember when I was a child, I didn't have a real Barbie house like most of my friends. I did eventually, but for some years I didn't. I remember loving the playdates at my friends' houses who had the whole pack, the house, the shop, the mansion. At that time, I used to cut the furniture from catalogues and put it on empty shelves in my room, I made their clothes with old fabric and Sellotape and created what felt like a cute home. Don't get me wrong, I also really enjoyed the original holiday convertible van from Mattel that I got one Christmas, but I can see how I learnt more and developed more skills when everything was not taken for granted, not delivered on a plate for my amusement.

I often worry that my kids have too many toys. Is the overload of options taking something away rather than helping them? Are we stopping them from being creative because they never get to be bored? I am sure that is not a worry I carry alone.

As part of my very natural concerns around 'do my kids have too many toys or not enough good ones?' and my obsession with gender stereotypes in childhood, it was only a matter of time before I came across the website of Let Toys Be Toys. It is a parent-led organization that lobbies and campaigns for a more inclusive way to understand toys; they have a lot of resources for teachers, parents, toy sellers and manufacturers and they are committed to stopping the gender segregation in the toys industry – and making sure our kids have as many options as possible. As a bonus, they even have an annual silliness awards where they highlight the worst examples of gendered marketing – last year the winners were the pink earth globes for girls and blue bibles for boys!

One of the great resources they have is an analysis by Early Years practitioner Leanne Shaw that reveals how different kinds of toys[55] help certain developmental areas, and why it's vital that boys and girls are encouraged to take part in all kinds of play. It will come as no surprise that while toys aimed at boys encourage activity and adventure, many girls' toys send the message that life is all about appearance and caregiving. I don't think I can explain this any better than Leanne does so, with her permission, I've included a direct excerpt of this below:

Outside

Bikes and other ride-on toys help develop strength in leg muscles, stamina and co-ordination. They develop balance, the concept of speed and space, and how to control our bodies. These are all physical elements. Some mathematical elements are also included, such as spatial awareness, and some personal, social and emotional elements, including perseverance and self-confidence.

Water play is great fun. It encourages exploration, cause and effect, and initial concepts of weight and volume. Children get more from water play if they play together, developing social skills and language and communication.

Home corner

Kitchen and cookery toys help to develop imagination and language, as well as a simple beginning to symbolic representation. If other kids or adults get involved it also sparks elements of making relationships, as it involves playing together, sharing, turn taking, etc.

Role play and dressing up

Both boys and girls enjoy dressing up and using their imagination. They often replay things that they have seen in their home life, on TV, problems they need to solve, or situations that are troubling them.

Younger children learn self-help skills, including getting the dressing up clothes on and off. Buttons, zips, Velcro and sleeves all offer challenges to young children, and this is the perfect opportunity for them to learn how to cope with them, without the pressure of having to do it for real, where time constraints often mean parents do these complicated things for them.

Older children improve social, planning and language skills, as they create a story.

If girls are offered only princess clothes to dress up in, they will only act as princesses. They will be limited in their imagination, not having the opportunity to problem-solve how to put out the fire as a fire fighter, or to bandage up a limb as a doctor.

Children naturally like to imitate the adults around them, especially their parents or primary carers. What could be more natural than a child pushing a buggy like Daddy, or rummaging through a bag like Mummy?

Jigsaws and puzzles

They teach fine motor skills, problem solving, the self-esteem gained from successfully completing a puzzle, and the enjoyment of working one-to-one with a parent or teacher.

Construction

In toy stores and advertising, building and constructing seem to be marketed almost exclusively to boys. Physical elements like fine motor skills, expressive arts and design, skills of imagination, mathematical skills of problem solving, as well as language development are all covered when building.

Children build tall towers, make plans and decide how to carry them out, and try and re-try when things do not go according to plan. Why steer girls away from these opportunities? They enjoy these activities and need to learn these skills too.

Small world toys

Cars, Playmobil, animals, dinosaurs, etc. From playing with these, children develop so many skills. They use imagination, language, finding out about the world, and maths, when they discover that cars roll faster down the ramp if it is steeper, or sorting all the farm animals into one group and zoo animals in another.

Young children don't make any distinction between these toys. There is no reason, in their eyes, why a Sylvanian family figure, an Action Man and a Barbie can't sit in the car and drive really fast away from the scary dinosaurs.

Reproduced with the permission of Leanne Shaw and Let Toys Be Toys

Source: https://lettoysbetoys.org.uk/resources/toys-and-learning/

When you think about toys as learning tools, and when you get a bit deeper into the skills they reinforce, it is very easy to see that all of them are necessary, and that every child would benefit from them all. By dividing types of toys by gender we are limiting skills for everybody. As we have seen already, these same limits are also pushed in every other aspect of their life, and if we think back to the 'use or lose it' concept, it becomes obvious this doesn't come without consequences.

It is not as obvious, as natural, or even as timeworn as we might think. The 'pinkification' of products aimed at girls and the unnecessary division that colour coding provokes are relatively recent. Advertisements from the 1970s showed kids playing with a variety of toys in bright colours like red, green or yellow. By the 1980s and 1990s, however, toys started to become more gender segregated but still nothing like the segregation of pink and blue aisles of today. It's simply and sadly just the result of clever marketing, with toy manufacturers and marketeers realizing that a lot of families bought twice as many things if they felt that what they had was not appropriate for siblings of different genders.

There is a now an assumed colour coding rule understood by both adults and kids in which everything pink is aimed at girls only. And the problem of that pinkification is the stigma that comes with it. No other colour carries that amount of alleged meaning. Nobody would deny the use of green or yellow to half of the population. Pinkification narrows choices and promotes segregation.

The first recourse of marketeers to get girls interested in toys that are culturally perceived as masculine is to launch a pink version of them! Pink gives them permission to embrace it. That same colour is a clear boundary for boys – if we want a boy to play with a toy perceived as feminine, we need to erase the penalty that pink carries. When we approach the segregation with 'Let's create a kitchen oven in a colour that boys can play with' we are reinforcing the problem, instead of creating a solution, because it perpetuates the (illogical) idea that colours have a much deeper meaning than they actually have. Those short-term solutions feed a marketing strategy that is damaging. The question we should be asking is not 'what is wrong with pink for girls?' but, instead, 'what's wrong with pink for boys?'. What is right or wrong with any colour at all?

We might feel that it is not that bad, but we just have to look around and stop and think about what we see in toy shops, in catalogues, in gifts for kids. What we can see in kids' behaviour. I am always fascinated about what we can discover from research and behavioural studies. They are never perfect, because of course you don't have a control group that hasn't been subjected to stereotypes, but there is so much learning that comes from observing things from a different optic.

In a study carried out with over 300 students,[56] researchers identified more than 100 toys and classified them based on how much each toy was associated with boys, girls or neither. It was found that girls' toys were associated with physical attractiveness, nurturance and domestic skills, whereas boys' toys were rated as violent, competitive, exciting and somewhat dangerous. The toys most likely to be educational and to develop children's physical, cognitive, artistic and other skills were typically rated as neutral or moderately masculine. It confirms that strongly gender-typed toys are not the best for an optimal development, and it is a very easy thing to check when buying toys. Who is this aimed for? Why? What kind of characteristics does it encourage? Is that characteristic something we want to foster?

But what happens if my kids want those toys? If they really, really want them? Once again, critical observation can answer that question. Do kids really want those toys or is that desire learnt?

In one experiment,[57] researchers took very similar toys that kids had not seen before and put them in stereotypical girls'/boys' boxes and gave them to a group of children. Both girls and boys explored more (and remembered more detailed information a week later) about the toys from their 'matching' boxes. Those were similar and novel toys for them. Another experiment showed that when they see a peer of their own gender playing with a toy, they categorize it as 'correct' and pay it more attention than when seeing the same toy being played with by a child from the opposite gender.[58] Kids are detectives, they find the clues that give them the information that they have learnt to identify as relevant. They know that their 'gender tribe' is important. They know which one they belong to, so they look for the rules to be good members of that group and conform to them. Don't we all?

Professor Lisa Dinella, Principal Investigator of the Gender Development Laboratory, at Monmouth University, Arizona, USA points to studies they have carried out whereby they encourage kids to play with toys which have obvious gender cues removed (e.g. colour) or they let the kids think no-one is watching them. Both scenarios effectively remove the social cost. Interestingly, when this is the case, they are much more likely to cross over the stereotypical boundaries. This is great news; we just need to bring it into real life!

The fact that kids understand, from an early stage, that there is a social cost for liking/choosing specific kinds of toys is very revealing about just how many of these preferences are not as free as we like to claim. This understanding of where that preference comes from allows us, as carers, to intervene a bit more without feeling that we are failing them. I am not talking about banning some toys or forcing others (although there are toys directly banned in our house, like guns or heels), more just proactively encouraging and presenting different options, celebrating the difference.

One of the most fascinating experiments made on toys was about not only the interest but also the ability to play with a game. Every gender not only liked better but also played better at a game (scoring higher) when they thought it was aimed at them.[59] That finding was a big 'of course' moment for me, and made me think about the impact it has in most sports, in which being accused of 'throwing/playing/running like a girl' seems like the ultimate insult. Girls not only see themselves less (if anything at all) in the media playing sports, but they are also made aware, from very early stages, that sports are more for boys (who, as we will see, also get better equipped to practise them in their daily wardrobe). The impact of this means there is less interest in sport, and that girls' playing performance is affected – which discourages them from participation. Then observers justify the lack of sportswomen represented in media with a 'they are naturally worse and it is boring to watch'. Physical considerations aside (and keeping in mind that a lot of sports rely very much on technique as well), how are we supposed to fix the gap in sport interest if all our justifications enlarge it?

That is the most fascinating (also, overwhelming) aspect of the whole gender stereotyping vicious circle. Unless you look at it globally, every small thing feels exactly like that, 'just a small thing', nothing to worry about, something perfectly innocent and natural. But when you start to put the pieces together, each of them a tiny part of a much more important narrative and reality, then it becomes frightening. Because those small things are more linked than they might at first appear, and they have a much bigger consequence on who we are inviting our kids to become.

Kids spend a lot of time playing (as well as reading and watching television, which as we now know are also full of gender stereotypes) so once again it is important to minimize how much we allow those toys/games to limit and take away free will on one hand, even if they are developing a skill on the other. The solution relies on variety and real choice. 'Real', that's the key, which in a world of smart marketing is not as easy as it would seem.

But again, it's not all doom and gloom. Things are changing. Initiatives such as Let Toys Be Toys and their relentless campaigning for a more gender-neutral approach to toys have already made a very positive impact. In the UK, physical shops have moved from an average of 50 per cent to almost zero signposting for boys'/girls' sections within their stores. Online, there was a 70 per cent drop in boys' and girls' categories in the four years following the start of their campaign in 2012. They are pointing fingers at the people making money out of the segregation and inviting parents, as consumers and educators, to take action. I can't repeat this enough: we have a say, we vote with our money and the decisions we make at home. We are educating a new generation and we have the possibility (and, I might suggest, the responsibility) to go a bit further.

We, as adults, need to ensure that all children get the opportunity to experience all different types of play, all different types of toys and all different types of friendships, rather than simple gender segregation. That means being aware as carers that there is no such thing as boys' or girls' toys and that our perception of 'my kid just naturally prefers this' is not as objective and natural as we might think. We need to be aware that stereotypes, especially with the help of marketing, have their tricks. It's our job as carers to make sure we too have our own tricks to remove those ingrained biases and the limiting effects that come with them.

Expert interview: Tessa Trabue

Speaking on behalf of Let Toys Be Toys.

Let Toys Be Toys is an award-winning social media campaign challenging gender stereotypes in childhood, especially in toy marketing, publishing and education. The campaign has success-fully convinced 15 major UK toy retailers to drop 'girls' and 'boys' signs from the toy aisles and let children have the freedom to choose things that interest them most, free from gender stereo-types. Tessa Trabue joined the Let Toys Be Toys campaign in early 2013 after being inspired to act when seeing the negative effects of gendered marketing on her young child. She is a founding member of the campaign's offshoot Let Books Be Books, which has persuaded 11 UK children's publishers to drop gendered labels on books, and of the campaign's Toymark award scheme, which celebrates UK retailers that model good practice in marketing to children.

When was Let Toys Be Toys born and why was it important enough for you to come from a thread to the impactful grassroots that it is now?

Let Toys Be Toys was launched off a Mumsnet thread in 2012 by parents who were fed up of seeing 'girls' and 'boys' signs in the toy aisles, which were present in 50 per cent of UK toy shops we surveyed at that time. When gendered signs are used to categorize toys, we find the same stereotypes repeated time and time again: action and adventure, construction and science toys are labelled for boys, while arts and crafts, cooking, cleaning, and caring toys such as dolls are signposted for girls. Play is crucial to how children develop and learn about the world, and we could see that these signs risked limiting the possibilities and interests of our children by telling them that certain types of toys or play were off limits to them. Studies show that by early primary-school age, children have already formed ideas about the different jobs suitable for men and women that can be hard to shift. These stereotypes can then influence subject study and career choices – we see a persistently low number of women choosing STEM careers along with small numbers of men taking up careers in the caring sector.

The campaign tapped into a groundswell of support from the public who shared concerns about the limiting and possible long-term effects of this gendered toy marketing, and retailers responded positively to our asks. Our survey in 2016 revealed virtually no 'boys' and 'girls' signs up in the toy aisles in the UK, and a 70 per cent reduction in gendered navigation online. Our subsequent Let Books Be Books campaign, launched on World Book Day in 2014, won wide support among authors and achieved similar success, with 11 UK publishers agreeing to ditch the gendered titles.

Although the overt 'girls' and 'boys' signs are mainly gone, gender stereotypes remain in other ways that toys are marketed to children. We see them in adverts, toy catalogues or even on the toy packaging, and we continue our campaign asking both retailers and toy manufacturers to market toys in more inclusive ways, such as using images of both boys and girls.

During your research and journey, what was the biggest WOW moment you had, or what was the piece of research that had the biggest impact on you?

Most of the Let Toys Be Toys campaigners like myself grew up in the 1970s and 1980s, experiencing a very different sort of childhood than the rigid pink/blue marketing divide we see today. It was common for brothers and sisters to share hand-me-down clothes and multi-coloured toys, and we came to the issue with a sense that the current pink/blue marketing wasn't the way things had always been done. Dr Elizabeth Sweet's research looking at toy catalogues from the early 1900s to the present day found that toys are actually far more gendered today than at any point over the twentieth century. Her research findings were a real eye-opener in confirming what we were up against in terms of the current extreme gendered marketing, and that we weren't challenging 'the way things had always been done' but something new altogether.

In terms of parents as principal educators, if you were to give them two or three practical things that they could start doing right now at home about gender stereotypes and toys, what would those be?

- Offer children options for different types of play and, when possible, a chance to play with a wide range of toys. As we found through our own research, it is more important that children are allowed the freedom to play with the toys that interest them, rather than being directed to certain types of toys.

- Challenge gender stereotypes when they come up. 'Why can't boys like pink? All colours are for everyone!' 'Lots of girls and women love football.' 'Why can't boys play with dolls?' 'Of course women can be astronauts.' Show examples to counter the stereotypes: watch a women's football game together; research a famous female astronaut; or play a game counting how many dads you can spot taking care of their babies while out on a walk. Have a look at our #caringboys, #girlslovespace and #morealikethandifferent hashtags on social media for lots of examples.

- Use your spending power and voice as a consumer. Retailers and toy manufacturers care what their customers think, and your opinion matters to them! Tell them what you like and what you'd like to see changed by speaking to shop managers or writing emails. And show the kids how to do this, too – many of the positive changes we've seen have been led by children. For a list of UK toy and book retailers which are smashing stereotypes, see <http://www.lettoysbetoys.org.uk/toymark/>.

For those parents wishing to learn more about the importance of toys free of gender stereotypes, are there any particular websites (as well as your own, of course!), books, videos, podcasts or other resources you would recommend to help them?

- Raising children without gender stereotypes – Dr Finn Mackay: <https://www.lettoysbetoys.org.uk/resources/raising-children-without-gender-stereotypes/>
- Beyond the Pink and Blue Toy Divide: Dr Elizabeth Sweet TEDx talk: <https://youtu.be/xdHJGH97vyo>
- *The Gender Agenda: A First-Hand Account of How Girls and Boys Are Treated Differently* by parenting duo Ros Ball and James Millar: <https://www.newsfromnowhere.co.uk/page/detail/The-gender-agenda/?K=BDZ0028997343>
- Unlimited Potential: The final report of the Commission on Gender Stereotypes in Early Childhood with recommendations for parents, teachers and retailers: <https://www.fawcettsociety.org.uk/unlimited-potential-the-final-report-of-the-commission-on-gender-stereotypes-in-early-childhood>
- Girl toys vs boy toys – the experiment: <https://youtu.be/nWu44AqF0iI>
- Why it's important to let toys be toys: Dadblog <https://dadbloguk.com/why-its-important-to-let-toys-be-toys/>

We also have a range of resources and blogposts at https://www.letttoysbetoys.org.uk on the importance of challenging gender stereotypes in childhood, along with practical tips for parents.

If you take away just a few key points from this chapter, let them be these

1 Toys help kids to learn. Different toys enhance different skills. We don't want to limit them but give them a bigger frame.
2 A pink version of a perceived-as-masculine toy doesn't solve the problem but aggravates it, as it reinforces the colour coding and the idea of natural interest/differences.
3 Same things apply when avoiding pink for boys at any cost. The demand to have a perceived-as-feminine toy in other colours before a boy can play with it reinforces problems.
4 When the gender cues and the social cost are deleted, kids play with a wider variety of toys.
5 Not only do kids like a toy/game better when they think it is for them, but they also perform better at it. By making everything for everyone we can unlock more potential.

What to do next

- Diversify the toys. I am not talking about throwing out or banning things, but about having an understanding of the toys around kids and see what else they could add. Are they offered a variety of things? Is there a default kind of toy that is gifted at Christmas and birthdays? Can we introduce new things that might bring something else to the table?
- Remember that you have a say as a consumer. You can go as 'activist' as you want if this topic touched a nerve. You can participate in campaigns, sign petitions and be on top of what different grassroots organizations are doing to change things. But if that is not for you also remember that, ultimately, we have a say as a market. By not adding to the lucrative reasons for splitting toys by gender and, instead, supporting the toys that fight those limitations, we are sending a loud message to manufacturers.

- Play something counter-stereotypical. Kids want to play with adults, and they can be easily convinced to try new things if it is presented as a fun and joint thing. If we, as a family, are comfortable playing with everything, that will be their normal.
- Talk to them. If they say that a toy is not for them, have the conversation. Ask what is stopping them, explore why they don't think it's fun, ask them what they like about the games and toys that they do like playing with. Giving them the tools and the frame to get out of their 'default' line of thinking is, most of the time, all the encouragement they need to try new things in a confident way.
- Encourage a diversity of friends. Have playdates with different kids, encourage mixed groups rather than single gender friendships. Segregation by gender starts very early and accentuates the power and rigidity of stereotypes by creating an *us/them* situation and mindset.

6

Clothes

When you get pregnant the very first thing people ask you is the sex of the baby. I myself sometimes ask pregnant friends if they are going to 'find out'. A lot of people choose not to know, they want the surprise (I personally think that the day is already full of surprises, but that's just me), and others are really eager to find out.

What I find really interesting is that a lot of people that choose to know do it because they think it's more practical, they defend their decision (not that they have to) as a useful thing that allows them to start buying clothes and preparing the nursery. They talk about the importance of being prepared, as if any of the things that you actually need for the arrival of a new-born are sex-related.

I have a boy and a girl and their bodies were extremely similar when they were born, one a bit taller, maybe the other one a bit fuller, but the same squeezable bundle of flesh and love. The only thing that was evidently different was their genitalia, but even that was not physically important enough to make gendered nappies a need. Isn't it funny that we are ok with unisex nappies, but we expect everything else to be different when, if anything, it should be the other way round?

Unsurprisingly, as on most occasions when binary gender stereotyping creates differences in that which is catered for, girls get the worst part of the deal. You might be thinking that girls' clothes are much cuter, and I agree, they are! But we are not dressing babies in cute clothes to do them a favour, we are doing it because *we* like it. We are the ones enjoying buying the clothes, seeing our kids in them, even folding them. We do it for ourselves. Your two-week-old baby doesn't notice if the pyjamas have flowers or trucks; she notices only whether the fabric is soft and cosy, whether they are warm, or uncomfortable; the band on the hair with a big flower is not for her comfort, it's for people to admire the way she looks. She's still a tiny baby but, once the weeks start to pile up, the differences start to matter more.

I remember a time when I wasn't a mother yet (although I was desperately trying) and I had a conversation with a friend about how hard that afternoon had been for her, trying to get her son out of the shoe shop without buying a pair of pink and glittery trainers. They had to hide them, ask the shop attendant to pretend there were none in his size, there were tears and tantrums and eventually he got a pair of navy ones. I wasn't in that moment as intensely critical and aware about the topic as I am now, but I found it shocking even then. 'Why didn't you just buy the shoes, if he needed a pair and he liked those?' I naively asked and I remember that she told me that I would understand better when becoming a mum myself. 'It is very easy to let your girl wear boyish things, but it is not the other way around, you will see.' I probably nodded and made a mental note to prove her wrong. I suppose I now have (not that she knows or cares), but yes, with all the pressure, it's not always easy.

I know this chapter is not going to be everyone's cup of tea. I know that there are cultural factors to consider, and that predispositions are so strong that no matter how well I present the facts of the existing research, a lot of people, even some hard-core feminists, are still going to feel uncomfortable with their sons wearing a dress, or wearing pink. They are going to get upset if their daughters are mistaken for boys by well-intentioned adults, or they are going to feel defensive because they find a lot of joy in seeing their kids dressed in a certain way, even if it stereotypes. Whatever you choose to do is ok, it's nobody's business but yours, but, because I am an optimist, I am going to try to convince you anyway.

I have to state that I practise what I preach and Eric himself wears dresses sometimes (not that my father loves it). He doesn't wear them most of the time but sometimes he does. Until very recently he was completely unaware that society was not ok with it, now he thinks it was just 'some of the older kids in that playgroup'. Nora is mistaken constantly for a boy; we are ok with that too because in the big scheme of things (probably even in the small one as well) it doesn't matter. What people think of your kids in their heads has no capacity to harm them (not that mistaking their gender should even be considered harmful). As far as I am concerned, people have sometimes confused me (I am Spanish) for Portuguese or Italian and I give it the same importance: I correct them if I can be bothered, I ignore it if not and in both cases I don't give it any moral weight.

My husband and I are ok with letting our kids choose their own clothes and sometimes they look more stylish than if we had chosen them ourselves, other times it looks like the wardrobe has vomited over them, and on both occasions they get dirty in a matter of minutes. On none of those days are they less boy, girl, or anything in between than others, nor are they smarter, kinder, funnier or more curious. The only difference on those days is how cute *we* or other people find them; well, that and how comfortable or limited they are by their outfit. Letting them choose their clothes empowers them to be themselves and gives them a say in how they are presenting to the world; it reinforces body autonomy (becoming a very easy way to teach them some personal boundaries) and for those that just want the practical angle, it also saves a lot of time in arguments – I'm learning that in the parenting game you need to pick your battles!

One of the things to remember here is that the choices are limited. Of course, we decide what we have in the house to start with and we normally buy (or select from hand-me-downs) what we are ok with them having in their drawers and what, for whatever reason (material, messages, shape, etc.), we don't agree with and doesn't make the cut. It is no different than the baby-led weaning method of starting kids on solids, the kids get to choose but only between what is offered. If you feel really strongly about your son wearing pink, then just don't have pink things (hopefully this will change by the end of this book, and it will be other things you will avoid).

If you feel that you can't deal with the judgement from people thinking that you are the monster that combined those patterned trousers with that *also* patterned t-shirt then just make stickers that say 'TODAY I CHOSE MY OWN CLOTHES' and enjoy how every stranger goes out of their way to compliment your child on their choice.

If it is still not doing it for you, there is another important thing to remember: these are short-term choices. They are not getting a tattoo, not even cutting their own hair, they are not deciding their future or moving to another country. They are putting some clothes on for a very short period of time – at most a matter of hours – so enduring the visual horrors of striped leggings mixed with a flowery t-shirt is not really a big ask. The thing here is that although your child's choices are short term, the messages they receive regarding what is encouraged or discouraged are long term. The limitations regarding the gender (that are already present in everything else around them) are part of a much bigger problem. What we tell them through their clothes, the choices or the lack of them, has a bigger impact than a neighbour thinking that we are colour-blind or lack fashion sense. Even if it wouldn't be my favourite outfit, I realize that the damage of pointing out 'Eric, that is for girls' will have a much longer effect than letting him bounce around in his Minnie Mouse dress. What I do say, and I say it to both of them, is, 'Are you sure you are not going to be cold?' or 'Are you sure that you are going to be ok on the bike with that?' or whatever rational reason that makes me think that their choice might not be ideal for the particular occasion.

There are different things that we can analyse when thinking about kids' clothes and their segregations by gender, things that we can be aware of just by paying attention when browsing in kids' clothes shops.

Colour

This is the first difference we spot when analysing differences in kids' clothes. The biggest and obvious one is the pink vs. blue, though it is also important to note when introducing different colours that girls' clothes tend to be pastel, while boys' colours are brighter. Although most parents will say that these colours are their children's natural choice, this segregation is a clear example of nurture winning over nature.

Until quite recently (compared to how long humans have been around) there was not such a thing as gendered colour. Even in the last century children used to be dressed in white (for ease of cleaning) and the literature shows that depending on the region and the times, pink and blue for boys or girls would vary. For example, a 1918 article from a trade publication called 'Earnshaw's Infants' Department' clearly states that 'Pink is for the boys, and blue for the girls. The reason is that pink, being a more decided and stronger colour, is more suitable for the boy, while blue, which is more delicate and dainty, is prettier for the girl.'

If you think about it, for the last 700 years the Virgin Mary has been represented in art dressed in blue and, as a baby, Jesus has been occasionally dressed in pink, as the pastel version of red, the colour which Jesus is typically wearing in the paintings.[60]

After the Second World War there was a huge swing from blue to pink: 'Rosie the Riveter traded in her factory blues for June Cleaver's pink apron,'[61] and we see around that age a lot of female moments packed up in pink (Jackie Kennedy's Chanel dress, Marilyn Monroe's outfit, etc.). Jo B. Paoletti, historian and author of *Pink and Blue: Telling the Girls From the Boys in America*, believes the line was more firmly drawn in the 1980s, when 'it became more and more common for parents to find out the gender of their children while they were still in the womb. Excited moms and dads wanted to buy gender-specific items for their new little bundles of joy, and of course, retailers obliged'.

If it were 'natural', you would expect to see pink preference from the beginning, but a large study of children aged 7 months to 5 years showed the opposite. It is only by the age of 2 that girls start to choose pink objects more often than boys. By the age of two-and-a-half, girls have a significant preference for the colour pink over other colours and, at the same time, boys show an increasing avoidance of pink.[62]

This is a perfect example to understand the huge impact that stereotypes have on kids. It is undeniable that pink is the preferred colour of a lot of girls. Girls learn from a very early age that things in pink are tailored for them, they are offered things in pink, it is a very easy code for them to assume. Yet, we say it is 'nature' and 'a free choice' when girls choose predominantly pink things.

Slogans and designs

If colours are very obvious, the designs and slogans are not far behind in blunt stereotyping. The first thing to point out are the almost absurd slogans, the ones that it's hard to believe still exist, the likes of 'too cute for maths' or 'keep your daughters at home, heartbreaker in the making' or 'my daddy says I can't date until I am 30', and so on – that kind of messaging is obviously wrong on so many levels. Poundland launched a special kids' edition shirt for the football European Championships with the slogan 'goal digger' and some people find a girl wearing it hilarious.

The problem is that we are not only fighting those alarming slogans, the ones that trigger an immediate reaction in most people. In fact, when you look a bit closer, the messages behind the 'normal' ones are still astonishing. It doesn't take much research, literally just a walk to a couple of shops, to see that slogans aimed at boys focus on action, skill, aspirations and taking risks versus dreaming, being magical or the 'keep smiling' slogans which are common in girls' clothing ranges.

Emma Roomes, on her website pinkandbluereview.com, analysed slogans in her own experiment, going to three different shops and making notes. She noticed that boys were told to be 'cool', 'the future', 'awesome', and even tolerated to present as funny, cheeky rascals. Girls were told to be 'loving' and 'beautiful', and expected to be 'vapid', 'ditzy' or 'ornamental'.[63]

Even if it is true that very young children can't read themselves what is written on their t-shirts, the adults around them will still comment on the words and repeat them to the kids. And it is not only the words – the motifs also play their role in defining the interests of the children wearing them. Cars, planes, rockets and headphones are usually reserved for boys, and suggest a natural interest in complex mechanical objects. On the other hand, objects related to the household and sociability such as lipsticks, cups of coffee or tea, flowers or mobile phones are the girls' lot.

Even animals, surely an unbiased type of motif, have their own set of stereotypes to communicate. Animals featured in boys' designs are more likely to have prominent teeth and be predators, such as sharks, bears and dinosaurs. Such dangerous animals live outdoors in wild environments, fitting the image of what boys should be interested in. This sends a message to boys that being aggressive is a positive behaviour. Displaying bold behaviours invites boys to hold on to their bravery, their autonomy. Most of the animals depicted on girls' t-shirts are pets. Cute representations of smiling cats, panting (never barking) dogs or chubby bunnies are very common. When a predator does make its way into the girls' section, it is to appear in a cute version, with endless eyelashes, or in the baby version, with fluffy fur or a pink ribbon on its head. Wild animals are depicted in a domesticated, friendly manner.

The way the motifs are drawn also exhibits noticeable differences: the depicted girls' animals are generally drawn as cute or rounded, not respecting the scientific representation of the specimens, while the boys' animals are drawn in their correct proportions, in a more realistic manner. And if you want to go even further, it is worth noticing that the food that is shown on the garments is different, too. Girls' clothes tend to show sugary food (doughnuts, ice creams, cakes, etc.) or healthy options (vegetables or fruit) while boys' feature pizza, hot dogs, bacon, hamburgers, etc. A review of children's departments in nine stores found a massive difference in the offerings per gender. In general, when food is represented on boys' clothing, it is something higher in fat and salt content, and it is pictured with, or as, a cartoon character in motion. For girls, there's a lot less action but more pervasive food imagery.[64]

It's worrying that, if we think about it, we know that the t-shirt with the cupcake is for girls. Even if we see boys devouring cupcakes! I remember it shocked me how that obvious stereotype was hidden in plain sight, just unquestioned. When did we all assume that, even if they all like the same things to eat, only certain groups are allowed to display them on their garments?

The 'rules' with any motif can be altered but if, and only if, you make a clear stand about how you have transformed it, almost an overcompensated apology for daring to cross lines. For example, boys now get motifs with sequins (I am so glad they demanded to the point that companies now find it profitable), BUT they are always very masculine motifs, with bold colours and block fonts. Girls might get a t-shirt with pizza, but they have to pay the price and have it decorated with ribbons, glitter or lace.

Shape

Girls' and boys' bodies are not very different until they get to about 6 years old. Up until puberty, girls and boys are pretty much 'child' shaped with similar waist, hip and height measurements and most high street retailers have identical sizing charts for both.[65] This includes shoes (with the same 'standard' width), hats and, yes, even underwear!

Yet despite the similarities, the shapes and production of the clothes are very different. Especially in the toddler years, the boys' clothes have more pockets and their clothes take more into consideration the idea of fun and activity, with more leg room for bending your knees, for example, says Francesca Sammaritano, a childrenswear designer and assistant professor of fashion at Parsons School of Design.[66] Designers even use the same dress forms for both genders. 'The body is the same, size-wise. You're growing and developing in the same way until you reach six years, more or less.'

The shorts for girls are too short and their clothes, in the correct size, are much tighter. They know their bodies are different, but the way in which these differences are catered for is also completely different. The edging for a piece of clothing designed with a boy in mind is plain, but for a girl, from the moment they are born (literally, new-born sleepsuits), there are teeny-tiny bows, ribbons and scalloped edging around the neck and sleeves. Pants for boys are simple, while girls' pants always have ruffles, lace or once again the mini ribbons. Also – and I have done this test myself, trying both on Nora – boys' pants cover more. Some underwear for little girls (toddlers!) doesn't cover their whole bottom (and if you're a woman reading this, you know how uncomfortable it is having underwear that doesn't play ball!).

There are also differences in cut — boxier for boys, narrower and more revealing for girls. The clothes for girls are copying the trends for adults, it is just so cute to see mini humans dressed up as full fashionista adults, I get it, but that means slimmer styles, cap sleeves, shorter hemlines and less practical embellishments. They are not the clothes that you would choose, even as an adult, to have the experiences of a child: climbing, playing, jumping, painting ... they are clothes that invite the wearer to be passive, and beautiful, and girls get this reinforcement from the many 'ohhhhs' and 'wows' and 'aren't you the prettiest?' that they receive when wearing them. Clothing sold as 'for boys' is more likely to be child-like and designed for comfort and an active lifestyle, simple and utilitarian.

Girls' clothes are adorable and there is plenty of variety, to the point that it almost feels unfair how much of the space of the shop they take up in comparison with the boys' stuff, but the truth is that (unsurprisingly) they are far from winning when we focus on what really matters.

I don't want to finish this part on shapes without addressing that a lot of these issues are relatively easily solved by buying boys' pants or trousers for your daughter. I get that. But it wouldn't be fair not to address the big fear that there is about boys crossing the dreaded line to wearing skirts and dresses, and how hand-me-downs, from big sisters to little brothers, are controversial when they really shouldn't be.

If we go back a bit in time, we notice that dresses were common for both genders until the beginning of the 1900s. The main reason for keeping everyone in dresses was toilet training, or the lack thereof, making the changes much easier. Dresses were also easier to make with room for future growth, in an age when clothes were much more expensive than now for all classes. At around the age of 7, boys would get their hair cut and wear trousers for the first time, as a symbol of the boy's step towards manhood: 'breeching'.[67] Dresses for boys stopped being popular and are now socially penalized.

It is worth mentioning here too the cultural lenses. In a lot of non-western cultures traditional clothing for men is essentially some form of dress. Our perceptions of what gendered clothing is not only reinforces gender stereotypes but also carries a very 'western' perspective on what is 'masculine' and what is acceptable. We get our ideas of here and now and act as if they were universal truths.

You don't put your son in a dress, everyone knows that, it's a universal truth. Even if that dress is the same one that you loved your daughter in a couple of years ago. We don't, because we give a lot of value to a piece of clothing, and because clothes are a way of expressing identity and personality. But, if that is the case (and again, I am not saying that you have to buy your son a dress, I am just inviting you to ask yourself this question), what do we mean when we say that we treat our kids exactly the same? That we don't see gender? That we don't stereotype? What are the lines that are ok to cross in the name of equality and what are the ones that are too dear a price to pay in terms of society's response?

In western culture there is no second thought about girls wearing trousers, and they have been wearing them for certain work or activities since the 1800s, but let's not forget that it did not become commonly acceptable to do so in public until the 1960s.[68] Lots of women had to face the societal response, lots of women were judged and criticized for changing something that today just feels like straightforward common sense. Hopefully this is an optimistic way to see that maybe it is a matter of time for boys and men to be reclaiming their right to wear dresses if they want to.

Material

If you spend some time touching the garments when shopping around, it is quite clear that boys' stuff is just simply higher quality. The fabrics are thicker, sturdier and longer wearing. The clothing is less flimsy. It's also just plain warmer. Don't take my word for it, do the test next time you are out and about.

Material is probably the least noticeable field that promotes gender differences. That said, it still does, not only on the quality side, but on an unconscious level. Clothes for girls are covered with itchy tulle, sequins and glitter fabrics which communicate the idea that clothes for girls need to be pretty rather than comfortable or functional. Once again, it subliminally screams about the importance of girls' looks over their actions and presents them as attractive beings who dress to please. They get rewarded, through compliments, when aligning with that idea.

Another shocking use is the one made of fluffy fabrics. If they are to be found in the boys' section, the soft and fuzzy part of the garment will be on the inside, to make a jumper warmer for example. However, the fluffy fabrics are commonly used on the outside of the garments of their female peers, so the girl wearing the jumper not only doesn't take any of the pleasant feelings but it also makes it more likely people will touch her. It communicates the idea that girls should be pleasant to see and touch but, most importantly, it influences the way outsiders interact with them, because if something looks fluffy and soft, it asks to be touched.[69] I remember being shocked by this, because it totally applied to me! I would have engaged with a girl – showing my interest and admiration about her clothing by touching it, not realizing that from a very young age girls will be more touched than boys and will learn to consider it normal. I don't do it anymore, but I find myself naturally wanting to, which I still find both fascinating and angering.

Shoes

The last thing I need to speak about, while we're on clothes, is shoes. Every now and then there is media attention drawn to a parent who calls out a major brand on Twitter or elsewhere for the differences in their shoes, but apparently that is not enough. Brands keep dividing their shoes by 'boys' and 'girls' with the most stereotypical criteria and keep making shoes adapted for expectations of what children do. They assume boys will be out and about exploring, and they expect girls will be looking for shoes matching their beautiful dresses, while calmly playing. They design shoes that hold the ankles of the boy, that are sturdy and waterproof with good soles. Girls' shoes are not well padded at the ankle, and they are not suitable for outdoor activities or bad weather.

In the case of shoes, it is not only a subliminal message problem, it is a real health problem, as Let Clothes Be Clothes is campaigning to change. Podiatrists agree that ballerina shoes offer almost no support and the lack of shock resistance from the soles on some girls' shoes can cause damage to joints, as well as lacking arch support. To make it worse heels have now become part of girls' shoes, not only in their 'dressing up' version but in their everyday styles, with some of them starting from age 4, or even in the toddlers' section.[70]

My rule with shoes for Nora, which I can recommend, is asking myself the question: 'Would I let Eric wear these?' And everything that doesn't make the cut for him gets discarded for her as well. If you feel very strongly about your son wearing certain colours, or materials or motifs, you can ask yourself: 'Would I be ok with a boy wearing these same ones in plain black?' And if the answer is still 'no', because of the shape, then maybe it is a good starting place for making the decision for a girl.

So yes, clothes and shoes, another one of those things that is put down to nature, yet we keep shaping the choices, predispositions and expectations that kids have during their development.

I don't mind Eric wearing a dress if he wants to, and he loves his pink t-shirts – it is his favourite colour, after all! I know Nora is called 'wee lad' when wearing her brother's joggers but I also know that she is warmer and her knees more protected. I pick my battles.

What I always try to do is triage the hand-me-downs/presents and give away the stereotyped slogans or designs, anything with too many textures, and anything that doesn't feel comfortable or that may limit their movements. I make sure the selection of clothes that they have doesn't reinforce ideas that I am not comfortable with, and I try to think about the short-term/long-term effects of wearing the clothes. And mainly, I always try to remember that no matter what, they will be covered in milk, squashed blueberries or mud in a matter of minutes.

Expert interview: Janice Yu-Moran

Janice Yu-Moran is the Chicago-based founder of unisex children's brand Hello Society Kids. She left her job as a hospitality marketer, working in an industry (luxury hotels) that was devastated by COVID-19, to pursue a venture that addressed the pain points she experienced as a mother shopping for kids' clothes. As a mother to a daughter and a son, she struggled to find gender-neutral kids' clothes that felt both stylish and inclusive. She wanted to give her children clothing options in different colours and styles without being constrained by gender. With a mission to reimagine the way kids dress, the idea of Hello Society was born. The clothes are designed by a mother who wants our children to live in an inclusive and equitable world.

Why did you start your gender-neutral kids' clothes brand and why is the impact that clothes have on kids' development important for you?

When I had my daughter, I realized the problematic messages about gender that were splashed on babies' and children's clothes. Why is it that boys are strong like dad and girls are pretty like mama? The issue with gender-specific graphics and messages on kids' clothes is that they are reinforcing harmful stereotypes. The gender normative 'trucks for boys, ponies for girls' aesthetics we usually see in children's clothing shape our collective preferences and notions about gender. They're telling society which qualities are deemed masculine or feminine. As clothes are so closely related to the expression of somebody's identity, the stereotypes they can carry out have a strongly restricting effect on children's future opportunities, whatever their gender is. I want my kids to be seen and treated like the little bundle of potential that they are, regardless of their gender.

When I looked into gender-neutral kids' clothes, the existing gender-neutral and unisex kids clothing has one glaring commonality: oversized and loose-fitting designs. Hoodies and joggers are aplenty in gender-neutral fashion and some might say that the options available are misogynistic. The unisex movement, for the most part, has offered clothing that errs on the masculine end of the spectrum of fashion, thus pushing femininity to the side. This decision by retailers to avoid marketing feminine style pushes the notion that only masculine clothing is worth being worn by both genders. If we truly want to be progressive and inclusive, we need to include items from the entire gender spectrum.

I started Hello Society because I wanted to rise up to the challenge of redefining kids' fashion. I wanted to make clothes that break gender barriers and create a path where gender no longer dictates how kids should dress. I set out to make the clothes I wanted for my kids – clothes in all colours with empowering messages in styles that are timeless and versatile. Finally, children's clothes that are made to fit all kinds of lifestyles and identities.

During your journey and your experiences on the ground, what was the biggest WOW moment you had, or what was the piece of research that had the biggest impact on you?

My biggest WOW moment was when I researched the history of gendered kids, clothing and I realized that so many of the 'guidelines' that society has been following are arbitrarily assigned by retailers and marketers. I read from *Smithsonian* magazine that in the early twentieth century, baby clothes were white because it was easier to bleach and then, in the 1940s, marketers exploited post-war baby fever and randomly assigned blue to boys and pink to girls so that parents would buy more clothes. I realized that if there was greater awareness around how these norms came to be, people would be more conscious of their choices and perhaps not blindly do things just because that is how it has been. It was an AHA moment that I needed to educate parents and help them unlearn what they've been conditioned to believe.

In terms of parents as principal educators, if you were to give them two or three practical things that they could start doing right now at home about their clothes choices and how to approach the impact they have, what would they be?

- Don't look at clothing as gender markers. If your kid is too young to choose their own clothes, parents can buy clothing in a variety of colours and ignore the gender-normative colour wheel. If you have older children, let them be part of the shopping process so they can pick clothes featuring the styles, colours, graphics and slogans that resonate with them. This tells kids that fashion is a form of self-expression, not gender expression.
- Parents can pass down children's clothes from one sibling to the next regardless of gender. It's great for sustainability so that you don't have to keep buying more, and it sends the message that kids' clothes are for all children and that boys and girls aren't constrained to only certain clothes.
- Language matters. Parents can stop referring to clothes as 'feminine' or 'masculine' and describe clothes with the qualities that they are expressing. For example, 'that outfit makes you look very fun'. 'This shirt says you're an animal lover.'

> **If you take away just a few key points from this chapter, let them be these**
>
> 1 Shape, materials, colours, slogans, motifs, etc., they reinforce the idea that kids are different, they perpetuate stereotypes regarding their interests, their skills, their needs, their personalities ...
> 2 Clothes send a very clear message that the priority for girls should be the way they look. Boys get to be comfortable.
> 3 Allowing a kid to choose their clothes – from the pre-selected clothes that you agree with them – allows them space to explore how to present to the world and have more autonomy.
> 4 Shoes affect physical development of the children. Some shoes, mostly targeted at girls, are problematic beyond the gender stereotyping.

What to do next

- Choose five to ten items of clothes and shoes targeted at boys or girls and think what are the cues that make it obvious. How would it be weird for kids with a different gender to wear it? Why?
- Make a list of what is important for you in kids' clothes (comfortable, warm, stylish, sturdy). Then check how that looks, depending on the gender. If there are any differences, ask yourself which and why.
- Think about your own clothes choices. What do you value in the way men look, or women? What do you think it is ok to compromise on? What would make you uncomfortable if other genders wore it, and why?
- Follow the initiative #ReviewsForChange started by Sarah Priestley Turner of @ca_spaces. Leave a review on the site of the shop you bought from, so other customers and their own team can see it. Lead with the positive, highlight how much your son loved their pink sleepers, or how much your daughter is really enjoying their dinosaur hoodie. It shows that you, a paying client, don't need the labels.

7

Language

When I read the book *Parenting Beyond Pink and Blue*, by Christia Spears Brown, I was shocked by how important it was to remember to talk about 'a child' or 'a kid' when referring to children, rather than as 'boy' or 'girl'. That wasn't very long ago, we're talking about a few months, when I had already drafted the plan for this book, and I knew I wanted to address language. I liked the whole book and some things really stayed with me; most of them felt like reinforcement of what I already knew (which is a great feeling!) and extra ammunition in the shape of well explained research for some of my arguments. But this thing about 'girls' and 'boys' was so obvious and yet it was a blind spot for me before I read it.

We do constantly repeat 'boy' and 'girl', 'man' and 'woman', even though we know the words 'child' and 'person'. We do it because we are used to doing it, and we are used to it because we have been taught that it matters. Adding that distinction reinforces, almost unnoticeably, the idea of genders being really important, as well as perpetuating a binary way to perceive people. Since then, I always notice when I hear myself or someone around me saying 'good boy' or 'clever girl' and all the possible variations thereof, to my children. And let me tell you, now that I know about it, I hear it too many times. By making very clear that it is important, we are making an unconscious statement. We don't say, 'clever brunette' or 'clever left-handed kid' because we don't deem those as relevant. We don't clarify other pieces of information about the people we talk about unless it is relevant for the topic. Except for gender. For some reason we constantly clarify gender.

Now that I am aware, I spot it really easily and I have realized just how present it is everywhere. I still say it sometimes, but when I do I proactively correct myself and try to change it to a name, or to something gender neutral. Not because kids don't have gender, but because it shouldn't be the constant thing that they are separated by, divided by. I also still find myself surprised when Eric tells me 'a person did this'. I find myself feeling a gap in the information, almost as if a piece were missing in the story. I have to consciously remind myself that there is no gap, and I have to remember that looking for that piece, in most cases, is a matter of habit and conditioning. Looking for that piece is a perfect reminder of how ingrained stereotypes and the importance of gender are in us.

So yes, I agree, it is really difficult to unlearn and relearn. I am passionate about this topic and yet every day I find myself having to adjust things, to bite my tongue, to train my brain and to do better and to keep learning. But the good thing is that it is not about doing it perfectly, as much as it is about doing it better. Better than our parents (despite their best intentions), better than we did last year, better than yesterday. In this never-ending process to make the world a better place, including educating kids better, we will never get it perfectly right, but that doesn't make it less important to keep trying! So hopefully that takes a bit of pressure off, without discouraging us from trying to change things.

There are so many things to take into consideration when analysing the role that language plays in our kids' development, but to do so we have to start by giving it the importance it deserves. Language is the way we construct our thoughts, our ideas and our vision of the world. Language shapes the bricks of who we become. Words can shape the way we think about others and about ourselves and even the most subtle differences can impoverish or enrich our experiences.

When I was about 16, I went to see a psychologist because I was struggling with anxiety, and I remember she told me that I spoke really badly to myself. I would say things in the context of jokes, or as an apology, 'sorry I dropped it, I am so clumsy', and never thought more about it. I was just joking, but she was very serious. 'Imagine hearing bad things about yourself all day, every day. Even if you think you know it is a joke, you are hearing those things and it will shape the way you see yourself.' I still do it; I still use self-deprecating humour to bond with people, and when I realize what I'm doing it still brings back that really unpleasant and uncomfortable feeling I had in the session.

Because of that same uncomfortable feeling telling me that she was right, I don't let Eric or Nora say bad things about themselves. I make a clear difference between 'I acted wrongly' and 'I am bad' or 'that was silly' and 'I am silly'. I think those small things matter, because we are listening to ourselves 24/7 and better to get that right now rather than in 12 years' time with a mental health professional.

Gender stereotypes and language are linked from before we are born. Studies show that once the parent knows the sex of the child, they start to describe the way they move in the tummy differently. If the unborn baby is kicking hard they will be described as 'temperamental' or 'emotional' if a girl, and 'active' or 'future football player' if a boy.[71]

Once the kids are born and cry (as all kids cry!) the reactions are different when those cries are for a baby boy or baby girl.[72] A study that wanted to investigate how gender affected the meaning of cries in caregivers found that adults attributed low-pitched cries to boys (despite the absence of differences in pitch between boys and girls) and high-pitched cries to girls. And, what is more shocking, they felt that those presented as belonging to boys expressed more discomfort. Crying, the only language a baby knows, even if done in a completely identical way, is already affected by stereotypes. This can, once again, sound small and harmless but there is numerous research that proves that women's pain is consistently underestimated by doctors,[73] and, unsurprisingly, is even worse for black women.[74] A lot of those internalized beliefs, 'harmless' ideas or stereotypes become part of how we behave and unconsciously act when we are adults, and sometimes cost lives.

So, from the moment a baby is born, actually from before and obviously unintentionally, parents communicate and perceive things differently, and there are now numerous studies that are picking up all these nuances, giving us a clearer idea of what is happening behind our genuine belief that we treat every kid the same.

Different studies show that mothers are the ones that provide the majority of the language input[75] but also that they interact vocally more often with their infant daughters than with their infant sons,[76] and they also use more emotional words and emotional topics.[77] In a meta-analysis they saw that, across studies, mothers tended to talk more, use more supportive and negative speech, while fathers used more directive and informative language.[78]

Another study shows that fathers also sing attentively to, engage and smile more with their daughters, and acknowledge their sadness more. While interacting with their sons the words are focused on achievement, such as 'win' or 'proud', and they engage more deeply in rougher and tumble play.[79]

In a study done after visits to Accident and Emergency for accidental injuries, researchers saw that parents were four times more likely to tell girls than boys to be careful if undertaking the same activity again. Parents also used 'directives' when teaching their 2- to 4-year-old sons how to climb down a playground pole but offered extensive 'explanations' to daughters.[80]

Those small things, those extra words or the emotional charge in them, the specific way to direct actions, or the difference in assessing risks and transmitting them don't happen in a vacuum. They are both part of, and the result of, a severely gendered and stereotyped world. As we have seen in previous chapters, the same kinds of messages, ones that reinforce our belief of what is masculine and feminine, are everywhere. Also, as we explored in the very first chapter, those different experiences have an effect not only on our experiences in the world but also in who we become.

One thing that we notice in small kids (and also it is assumed in adults) is that girls speak better, speak more and speak sooner than boys. Even when I was speaking with my husband about this chapter, he was confused about me trying to justify otherwise, 'but we have seen it in our kids and our friends' kids, Virginia' as if that should be the end of the discussion. And it is true that there is some research-based evidence that shows that gender differences in language development, to some extent, reflect differences in the brain structure[81] as well as differences in the speed of developmental processes.[82] But those differences are quite small in terms of months of development. More recent authors also emphasize the importance of socialization and cultural factors in gender differences[83] and we can see that different interactions between parents and children (but also things like the kind of play that is encouraged in girls – role playing and symbolic play) can be more effective in promoting language ability.

So, as a meta-analysis of different studies[84] indicates, not only are the differences in language ability indeed quite small, but they also increase with children's age – just like many of the differences associated with gender. This again confirms the hypothesis that as well as a natural predisposition, there is a lot of nurture to account for.

The problem when we read articles/theories that support the differences in kids is that we use them as an excuse to allow them to happen without having to look any further. I was speaking with a speech therapist who told me that a lot of parents delay, or refuse altogether, to get their sons assessed because they just hold on to the idea that boys speak later. Using those stereotypical traits as an unchallenged truth stops us from correcting behaviours in time (for example, 'boys will be boys' or 'she's just a drama queen') or, in this case, can even stop parents seeking the professional help they in fact need.

Specific speech and language skills should be understood as developing within a range, rather than by an exact date (normally divided in to six-month chunks such as: between 12 and 18 months they should say one or more words; between 18 and 24 around 50 ...) and it is very important to keep an eye on those to be able to spot areas that might need special reinforcement. What happens normally is that the difference between a perfectly normal girl (in our case, Nora) developing her language skills in the early stages of the expected range and a boy, also perfectly normal (in this case, Eric), developing it in the later stage of the range, is really noticeable for parents, especially as we can't help comparing and looking for milestones. That brings a tricky parenting situation in which it is important to understand the slight physical (and cultural) gender differences without falling into the trap of ignoring signs when there is a problem that requires further assistance. How? By making sure that we are proactive in the stimulation and keeping an eye on the expected milestone ranges, all the while letting our kids thrive within their normal rhythms.

The last thing about language, which is nothing but the first thing I opened this chapter with, is the power of how our language carries unconscious stereotyping that we pass on and reinforce every day, and how small tweaks in the way we speak can play a big part in the way our children (and we ourselves) perceive the world.

There are extensive studies that analyse how different languages and their use of gender can reinforce and build gender stereotypes.[85] After analysing over 25 different languages in detail, researchers believe that the language you speak can shape your psychological stereotypes. The speakers who have stronger gender stereotypes in their language also have stronger gender stereotypes themselves. Countries with grammatical gender languages were found to reach lower levels of social gender equality.

For example, most languages use masculine generics, so masculine forms not only designate men but also designate mixed-gender groups or persons whose gender is unknown or unspecified. Feminine forms, on the other hand, refer to women only. That in itself is a very strong message to receive. Women (and girls) find themselves silently included in those masculine forms, and they adapt to something that doesn't necessarily fit them under the premise that it is neutral. Men don't ever have to compromise in the other direction.

In Spain, for example, if a classroom has 100 students and they are all girls, you would refer to them as 'alumnas', in the feminine way, but if one boy arrives in the class the 101 students would be referred to as a group, with the word 'alumnos' changing it to masculine, but with the understanding that masculine word is "neutral" in this case. But how is that neutral? And what subliminal message are we receiving with it? And how do kids receive that message when they are too young to understand the linguistic rules? They won't know or understand the explanation behind why that is the case, they will only know that as soon as a boy enters a group, the majority of girls have to adapt to a masculine language.

Gender-fair language was introduced in 1975[86] as a response to this structural asymmetry and it suggests two different ways to address the imbalance:

- Replacing masculine forms with gender-unmarked forms when possible (policeman for police officer, mankind for humankind).
- Using both masculine and feminine forms when it is not possible to find an alternative. Yes, even if it is too long sometimes.

When we use masculine generic terms, we tend to imagine men, even if we are referring to a mixed group or to an ungendered person.[87] The way we normally fix it is by clarifying that it is a woman when that is the case. We have CEOs and women

CEOs, we have football and women's football ... The problem with this approach is that we don't gender everything, only the counter-stereotypical things, and that still leaves us with many more men being visualized (for everything not specified) plus the reinforcement of the stereotypes. This sends a clear message of what is normal and what is not. We have male nurses and nurses, who are already presumed to be women, for example.

If, when we were speaking (not only with our kids but in general), we referred to male doctors, or the Men's Premier League, it would be a shock for those around us, because people don't expect to be reminded of gender when it aligns with their expectations. Doing so creates a certain discomfort and successfully leads some people to question themselves: why wouldn't I feel like this if it were the other way around? Also, if we did this and we started constantly seeing articles in the media about 'male board members, male tennis players, men scientists' we would quickly realize how extremely unbalanced the situation is in terms of exposure and power holding. Language is a powerful tool to shine a light on a problem, but it is also a great tool to hide it.

If we only point out the gender when it is unexpected, we reinforce the idea that the gender is important ONLY in those exceptions, we are receiving a message that the fact that she was a woman was very important in the context of her success, diminishing her position and putting her in a different frame.

The approach that would be much more effective in terms of critical thinking and societal awareness, when we can't find a gender-neutral way to express things, would be to point out ALL genders, rather than not pointing out any. If we don't point out any, the problem of the imbalance and expectations is kept invisible and untackled, and our brains keep perceiving that when we say nurse we are talking about a woman and when we say CEO we are talking about a man. And that is especially important for children, who will pick up quickly who needs the special labels in those circumstances.

Eric asked us the other day 'Why are there no men playing this game of football?' It makes sense because the classes he goes to on Saturdays are open to anyone and they are mixed, so it wasn't obvious to him that adult games are separated. He also doesn't know yet that men's football is what we would consider 'normal' football because it is the most watched and followed.

We explained that in sports sometimes the teams are men only, sometimes they are women only and sometimes they are mixed. But this was a clear realization that we should have talked about watching 'men's football' instead of using just football. That way, in his still developing phase, football (or anything where you apply this) would still be mixed until proven otherwise, and there would not be subliminal messaging about hierarchies, or what is universal and what is an extension. By using gender-neutral language and specifying gender in every case, when it is not possible or when further gender connotation is needed, we educate our brains and we perceive the world in a much fairer way.

What if kids grew up thinking that gender has to be specified only when there is a reason for it and the rest of the time it is assumed that everything is for everyone? How much better would the life of those children, especially non-binary children, be?

I just want to finish this chapter with a really good quote by writer Peggy O'Mara: 'The way we talk to our kids becomes their inner voice.' So let's use that power of language as a tool, let's give them a fair and empowering inner voice that's full of possibilities!

Expert interview: Kirstie Beaven

Kirstie Beaven is founder and editor of *Sonshine Magazine*, a quarterly publication dedicated to raising boys for a more equal world. A writer and editor, Kirstie has worked in educational settings and major public institutions for twenty years, creating content that makes ideas around art, identity, heritage and society accessible to as many people as possible.

Why did you start Sonshine, a magazine about raising boys for a more equal world through the challenge of gender bias in kids?

My first child was a daughter. I thought I knew a lot about how I'd raise her to challenge stereotypes and not be constrained by society's ideas about what being a woman was supposed to mean. However, after I had my second child, a son, only a couple of years later I realized there was so much stereotyping applied to boys, but (unlike the stereotypes applied to girls) no one was really discussing this in the parenting world.

In these first few years of having children I spent a lot of time with a writer friend of mine, Hayley, and as we watched our children grow, we had a lot of conversations about how the world was nowhere near as gender equal as we had thought it would become when were younger. We were looking for the missing pieces of the puzzle. Why was change so slow?

It seemed to us that society had been talking about gender equality as a 'problem' for women and girls, rather than a problem for all of us, and so men and boys were often left out of the conversations. Changing the world for boys as well seemed the only way to make sure we changed it for the girls too. We looked for the resources and articles about this, but they were few and far between, so we decided to start our own place for challenging stereotyping for all children, but focusing on parents of boys, who so often are missed out of the thinking around gender equality.

During your journey, reading and observations, what was the biggest WOW moment you had about language, or what was the piece of research that had the biggest impact on you?

I think reading Angela Saini's book *Inferior: How Science Got Women Wrong* when my children were very small gave me a real jolt. Particularly the chapters on early child development and how parents talk to their children so differently before they even turn one – it really made me think about how I might have been unconsciously creating a difference between them, even though I thought I was thinking about stereotypes!

But there is so much research available now to show how powerful our conditioning around language is. A 2014 paper from Katharine Johnson, Melinda Caskey, Katherine Rand, Richard Tucker and Betty Vohr, published in *Pediatrics*, December 2014, titled 'Gender Differences in Adult-Infant Communication in the First Months of Life',[88] showed this. They not only found that mothers talk more to their children than fathers do (using more words), but that mothers speak more, and respond more vocally to baby girls than they do to baby boys. I found this mind blowing. That as parents, we might actually speak less and respond less to a baby because of its gender.

In terms of parents as principal educators, if you were to give them two or three practical things that they could start doing right now at home about language and kids and how to approach the impact it has, what would they be?

My quickest fix is to stop grouping them as boys and girls. I notice myself how easy it is to slip into this as a parent in the playground, for example: 'why don't you go and play with those little girls on the swings?', or 'come on boys, let's go and have lunch now'. Children learn from us what is important in our society and we are constantly telling them how important we think that gender binary is.

Another simple change at home is to check that you are not applying gendered assumptions to jobs – use the gender-neutral term firefighter for example, rather than the default 'fire*man*'. Make sure you are not adding unnecessary gender descriptions too, no need to say female footballer or male nurse. They are just footballers and nurses.

Finally, I often swap around the pronouns in the picture books we have – you would be surprised to find how many books about animals refer to them all as 'he' or 'him'! We replace some of the male pronouns in classic children's picture books with 'she' and 'her', or 'they' and 'them'. I try to catch myself when we are talking about animals too – for example, not to gender the mini beasts we find in the park or garden. Partly because I don't want to reinforce our own societal stereotypes, but also because nature is much more various than we give it credit for. Some animals are hermaphroditic, some can change from male to female, and some do not need to mate to reproduce.

For those parents wishing to learn more, are there any particular websites, books, videos, podcasts or other resources you would recommend to help them?

There is a great documentary made by the BBC called *No More Boys and Girls: Can Our Kids Go Gender-Free?*. It follows a single class of 8 year olds and their teacher's efforts to change their stereotyping in their classroom. One of the key things the researcher/presenter changes straight away is how the teacher talks to the children. He calls the girls 'sweetheart' and 'love' while calling the boys 'matey' or 'sir'. Even this small change has a huge impact on how the children begin to see themselves.

I'd highly recommend Cordelia Fine's *Delusions of Gender* as a general introduction to how gender differences are not ingrained in our brains, and also the book *Inferior* by Angela Saini that I mentioned before, which gives a very readable introduction into how stereotypes affect our daily lives.

Of course, I'd also recommend that you read our magazine or find us on social media as these are exactly the topics we cover – we want to see this change for our children, more quickly than it did for us!

If you take away just a few key points from this chapter, let them be these

1 The way we normally speak, constantly indicating girl/boy, man/woman, reinforces the idea that gender is an important part of the story, and that it's a crucial category to divide people.
2 Gender stereotypes and the language used alongside are forced on us before we are even born. It carries a lot of stereotypes and presumptions.
3 Daughters have emotional intelligence reinforced through the way we speak with them, they are also invited to be more cautious and empathetic. Boys are given more instructions and are invited to be more competitive.
4 Different languages often use masculine forms even during times when the gender of a person is unknown or unspecified. That reinforces the idea, unconsciously, that masculine is generic, feminine is specific.
5 Language is very powerful. The way we speak and the words and language they learn to use will shape the way they speak to themselves and how they construct their world.

What to do next

- Be mindful of your language. And know that it will take a while to become natural, so expect a lot of self-corrections (we all have to do it all the time, with the new things that we keep learning).
  - If you don't know the gender of the person in the story, just use 'they'. 'Someone lost this umbrella, they must be looking for it.'
  - Use gender-neutral nouns when you can: folks, everybody, firefighter, police officer, house cleaner.
  - Avoid using man (or mankind) to refer to both men and women.
  - Try to use person instead of man/woman. Use kid, friend or child instead of boy/girl.

- ○ Avoid always using masculine when referring to animals that you encounter, from bugs to squirrels ...
- Language matters. Teach children proper names of their private body parts. Knowing real names is important in terms of safety and it also normalizes their bodies and empowers their relationships with it. There is so much power in words.
- Be conscious of the stereotypical adjectives, words and conversations that you have around kids. Are you praising beauty in girls and strength or speed in boys? Are you asking them the same kind of questions? Are you celebrating the same things?
- Now that you know the different encouragement that kids have to be wild, or assertive, or to express feelings, see if you are holding that unconscious bias. Are you using 'careful' more often with girls? Try just to describe the risk you are observing: 'this floor is very slippery'. Are you referring to them as bossy? Are you stopping boys from complaining and just telling them 'you are ok', 'you are a big boy now' or similar? Try acknowledging their emotion instead.
- A lot of the advice on how to be more gender neutral is to avoid the gender specification of roles. I agree with this, in general, but sometimes I actually find it much more powerful to specifically state the gender of the role when you're talking about 'the norm'. Start talking about 'men's football', 'men's golf', 'men-only panel' to create a thought-provoking immediate action. (Think about Natalie Portman presenting the best director category at the 2018 Golden Globes saying, 'And here are the all-male nominees'.) It is also a great conversation starter for curious kids.

8

Why it matters? Girls

Sometimes I look at Nora and I think about myself at her age. I think about all the girls. I think of us as a group – girls and women. In a world in which girls and women don't get dealt the same cards as boys and men.

It is amazing how babies become little people. I find myself looking at them surprised about how much of their own selves they are. How much they have changed in some things; how much they have stayed the same in others. It amazes me how much they absorb, they copy, they incorporate external factors into their uniqueness. How much all those little pieces of here and there are now part of them, and how many other pieces will come and go.

I look at Nora, laughing and running about, and, as well as feeling great pride, I can't help but be worried. I worry about how much of the care-free abandon is going to be stolen from her. I worry for the decisions, small and big, that are not hers but an amalgamation of other people's expectations and the unfair idea of what should matter to her. I fear subliminal scoreboards and the checklists that she is going to be measured against. I want to protect her from all of it, but I know I can't. So I choose instead to delay and minimize the inevitable and I try to equip her with the tools I wish I had had from the beginning.

Lately I have been trying a new thing that is really powerful. I try to live my life as I would like Nora to live hers. I find myself wondering 'what would I want Nora to do in this situation?' and then I try to lead by example. My life has improved a lot since starting this. I have let go of a lot of guilt from the 'selfishness' of setting boundaries or putting me first. I want Nora to put herself first in her own life, I think we all should. I want her to be kind and generous, but also to unapologetically say 'no' and own her decisions without the fear of paying the price in terms of likeability.

I want her to have a life of fulfilling experiences that she herself has chosen. But I know those choices will only be real if she knows that there is more than one path she can choose from. If she knows that she can design what being a girl and woman is, *for her*. That is why we need to broaden the choices when the world only points us in one direction.

The other day it was sunny in Belfast, for a change, and we rushed out of the house to go to the beach. I hadn't shaved and felt really uncomfortable with the idea of leaving the house with hairy legs, even if I have no problem with other people's body hair. But I did, I left with my unshaved legs because I don't want my kids to think that women always have to be hairless, because I didn't want them to see that our excursion had to wait for me to conform to some rules that I don't agree with in the first place. Because in order to be a choice for Nora, she has to see that it is also a choice for me, and sometimes I will do it, and that is ok, and sometimes I won't, and that it is also ok. She needs to see that body hair won't stop me from enjoying a day out having fun and eating ice-cream, so she knows it doesn't have to stop her either. You don't have to do exactly this, it's just an example, but of course kids are always watching and learning, so if we want to liberate them, we need to start with our own liberation.

When I discuss feminism with non-feminist women, they swear that they aren't worse off because of their gender. They tell me that they feel that they always had the same opportunities as boys and men, and sometimes they say that they had it easier. They are normally sympathetic to the horror stories that a lot of women talk about, but they refuse to believe that these stories are the norm because this has not been their experience as women. But it is the norm. Maybe not the horror stories, but the rest of the things that allow those horror stories to happen to women in the first place. And it is their experience, knowingly or not, since the moment the world considered them girls or women. Just because we are not aware of something doesn't mean it is not happening to us.

I got my ears pierced when I was a baby, just like most Spanish girls (at least of my generation). My parents never thought anything of it, it was the default, and I never thought anything of it either, so I presumed I'd probably do the same if I ever had a little girl. Chris asked me once if it didn't freak me out and my first instinct was to defend it – it was cultural, there was no harm in it and I didn't see the big deal. 'Think about it again, Virginia, little babies being pierced for an ornamental reason just because they are girls, without any capacity to consent,' and wow, the penny dropped. It was awful. But I didn't see it before. Even if I don't think about having my new-born's ears pierced as a traumatizing event, even if I don't blame my parents and even if it has caused me no harm, it is undeniable that I was affected by a culture that separates children into boys and girls and expects different things from each of them. To the point of piercing them, without consent, to look pretty for others. Just because I wasn't aware of the importance, it didn't mean it wasn't happening, or that it wasn't happening to me.

I hope that by now, after seven chapters, there is no doubt in your mind about the intense and harmful separation that these binary categorizations can present. Categories that create a sense of 'us' against 'them', along with the risks that this presents. Especially when one of those very recognizable groups holds much more power than the other.

I also hope that I've presented enough evidence and clarity about how stereotypes are everywhere and how they keep perpetuating the same (harmful at worst, narrow at best) messages. We now know how the lives of our children are different because we have seen how the media, the books, the clothes, the language and the daily stereotypes send very loud messages, even if as carers and educators we take pride in being all about equality.

But the question of this chapter is: *is it that important?* We are now a more equal society than ever before, so we must be doing something right; is it petty trying to change these small things? Are we, as some will argue, going too far? It is true that we are better now than ever, but we are better because of the people that fought the things that weren't fair, the small, the big and everything in between. We are better off because someone cared enough. So, when is it ok to stop caring? When is it ok to make peace with the differences because they are not as big as before?

Just because we got this far doesn't mean that things are fixed. It 'just' means that we are going in the right direction. I think we should use the energy from the victories that have got us this far and combine it with the action-inducing anger of the things that we have still to change, and make sure that we keep building a better world. We might not see the final result, in fact, let's be honest, our kids won't see the final result ... but shouldn't we aim to do even a little bit better? For those of you who are still not convinced about the need to change those 'petty' things, let me paint an example picture of the effects of gender stereotypes in girls.

So, let's imagine a girl, we'll call her Jane Doe. She leaves the hospital in her baby pink onesie, a big hairband with a flower adorning her bald little head. All the cards are pink, they welcome the 'princess' to the world with kind words and expectations. There are non-stop comments about how gorgeous she is, and about every little outfit she has (most of them full of gendered fluffy designs, most of them just a tiny bit more uncomfortable or unpractical than those of her brother, most of them also in any of the 50 shades of pink). She is sung nursery rhymes about mothers who care about everything (mother duck with her ducklings, mother monkey who calls the doctor, the mummies on the bus calming the crying babies) and about the usual stereotyped male roles (Old MacDonald and his farm, the Duke of York with his 10,000 men, the Humpty Dumpty's King and his men). While she starts growing, she is read books that make her see women as teachers, and mothers, she watches films in which she is a secondary character, where the female character is the one with the long lashes. A character who is beautiful and thin with impossible measures who she starts to see as desirable.

She is told that she can be anything that she wants, that the sky is the limit, while also being applauded the most for looking cute, for staying at the table quietly colouring instead of climbing around. She will be told to 'be careful' when trying new things and the boys around her will be told to stop playing rough with her, because we know how boys are, little brutes. Not like her, she could hurt herself. She will be told things like 'she is going to break hearts' or 'Daddy will have to stop the boys at the front door' from an insanely young age. I get it, it is a joke, a complimentary joke, but sit with it for a minute – isn't it a bit odd that little girls, as little as 2 and 3 years old, are complimented for a future of being sexualized by the way they are potentially going to look? Also, the confusing messaging we are sending when on one hand parents are scared of their little girls dating (heterosexually, because that is what we presume), because boys will be boys, but also, we get offended for assuming the worst in boys because #NotAllMen. I will pick this up in the next chapter.

She will go to school. She will be wearing her summery dress with socks, or the skirt with tights. Her clothes are not as comfortable to run and play, and she has already learned that there is shame in her body, that she shouldn't show her underwear ... so she plays with other girls while the boys occupy most of the playground. She will go to school and most likely do well, the school is an aseptic environment in which girls flourish, because it matches the skills that they have already been told to develop. Be kind, be nice, be quiet. Girls do well in school even if they are more insecure about some subjects, even if they don't see themselves as much in the history books, the English books, or science books. Girls do well in school for the same reasons that they don't do as well in other areas of life, because they play by the rules. They work hard, and they've learnt that by working hard you get fair reward.

'You can be anything, the sky is the limit.' But the world tells them, in every possible way, that getting married and having babies is the ultimate goal in life. We show them other girls dreaming about their wedding day, about their husbands, about their kids. The other women around them are carers, are amazing and loving women that happen to be carers, why shouldn't they want to be like their mother? Or their teacher Ms. Whatever, who is the sweetest adult, and also fun. Why shouldn't they measure happiness and ambition as being like the people they admire the most? We give them dolls to play with, and mini kitchens, and tell them stories with lots of mothers and teachers, and beautiful people. We show them female everything (from ponies to M&Ms) with long lashes, looking gorgeous. Why shouldn't they want to be gorgeous? Who doesn't like the 'wow, look at you, all beautiful' when entering a room? We are telling them that the sky is the limit but also presenting female success as a thin and beautiful mother/wife, with a career in the caring sector. There is nothing wrong with being that, with wanting that, but if our ambitions and choices have always been pushed in that direction, is it a true choice?

They can be everything, the sky is the limit for this generation. But they don't know the real names of their body parts and periods, and their normal bodily functions are still full of shame and taboos. They are sexualized and have been catcalled since the age of 11.[89] They learn to play this game of unspoken rules by ear. They know that men's approval and being liked by them is great – who doesn't want to be the popular girl in the class that all the boys like? Especially since we quickly learn from media how important it is for a girl to achieve status. But they also know that it feels dirty and wrong sometimes, and suddenly it's not only their classmates, it's older boys and men in the street.

It is only a matter of time, and that comes earlier than we think, before they learn about the options of being a 'slut' or being a 'prude', being the 'gross' one that no one likes (and who becomes the butt of the joke) or the one that is 'too full of herself' because she thinks she is pretty, the one that other girls must hate, because we also learn that women hate other women (even if, five minutes ago, we were forced to always be together). Women as the queen bee and the workers, the drama, the jealousy, the rivalry ... we see all that, we are fed all that.

So very soon they figure out that they have to be beautiful but without letting anyone know that they are trying to be beautiful because that is lame and shallow. They figure out that they have to be funny but not too funny, and never fart-joke funny. They feel the pressure to reject everything feminine that not that long ago was shoved down their throat; suddenly being feminine is the worst, it's cool not to be like the other girls. Who would want to be like the other girls, the way we are presented? Who wants to be the girl that cries 'like a girl'?

In their exhausting lifetime's search to reach for the sky that they have been promised, girls will be sexualized, interrupted, underestimated, ignored, ashamed, touched and objectified. They will spend a fortune and a lot of time on products and services that men aren't expected to want or need. They will dedicate a lot of time to look the way it is ok to look. The way they have been told it is okay to look. It doesn't matter if in the 90s it was 'heroin chic' or that it's now the Kardashians with impossible curves. We always believe it's our choice, we just happen to like it, all at once, and we invest in that. After all, we know for a fact that the world treats us much better when we look the part.

Everything is always on the edge with women and girls. There is always an expensive opportunity cost with everything we do, and the grey area feels unreasonably small. She is submissive or bossy. The pushover or the arrogant one. The superficial one or the one who let herself go. Either it is our fault because we don't talk enough, or it is our fault because we talk too much. We are stupid to walk home alone at night and what were we thinking of, or we are hysterical man haters who are taking things too far.

It is very difficult to educate our girls because we need to constantly empower them for the best but prepare them for the worst. We want them to be confident and brave but also want them to be careful. We have expectations about what being a girl and what being a woman looks like and we inevitably pass these expectations on to them. We want them to win and to thrive in that grey area, even if deep down we know that there is no grey area and it feels that we can never win, let alone have it all.

We leave the hospital with our pink-dressed bundle of love and we imagine ourselves developing the relationship that we think we would get by having a girl. We foresee scenes of happy times with our daughters. We imagine ourselves at their weddings, we imagine ourselves as grandparents, we imagine our feelings when they start dating (again, most likely assuming their heterosexuality), we imagine us proudly seeing them break the limits that the ones before them couldn't. We imagine them as the women that can finally have it all, the great partner, the kids, the high-flying career. And we tell them that if they study very hard, they will get it, and we tell them that they are every ounce as good as boys, and we make sure that they have big dreams.

But they will still today be most likely undervalued when applying for a job with a very good CV, because experimental studies have shown that an identical CV and application letter results in different perceived competence levels and job offers, depending on whether the applicant is identified as John or Jennifer.[90] She will most likely have high-level bosses that are men and who will tend to mentor and sponsor other men. It's not their fault she doesn't play golf. Every little bit just adding a little bit of extra friction to career advancement. Every friction feeling too petty for her to make a fuss about, who wants to be the angry woman? Nobody likes an angry woman.

If she happens to have a man as partner, she will work an average of seven hours more a week in unpaid household and care work in the house if they both work full time.[91] She will still most likely be the one doing more of this unpaid work even if she has become the main earner of the family.[92] She will be exhausted, and overworked, and most likely carrying most of the mental load of the whole family.

Ok, I think that's enough. I genuinely could go on and on. I could go further and analyse how different our lives are in school, in our teens, how differently we explore our sexuality, our career options, our experiences in the workplace, how differently our health problems are studied, or our pain rated. I could talk about the different exposure of our achievements in the media, or the different investment that all-women's projects get in venture capital (1p per pound, while all-men's get 89p per pound).[93] We can talk about how paternity affects genders so differently and how the expectations of motherhood are unreal and filled with guilt. I could talk about the dream gap, the pay gap, the pension gap, the glass ceiling, the sticky floor, the broken ladder.

We can be outraged about every single piece of evidence of inequality, trust me, I am! But we can also choose to change things from the very beginning. We can choose to not look the other way. We just have to start by acknowledging that there is a problem, a huge problem that, realistically, we can't fix (although let's not stop trying). And we can look at the new generations and make a vow to make things better for them, and also make sure they will make things better for the ones after them.

Expert interview: Hannah Wilson

Hannah is a former headteacher who taught English, Drama and Media Studies for 19 years in challenging urban schools in South London before relocating for a headship to Oxfordshire. Outside of the day job she co-founded a grassroots gender equality network called #WomenEd which is now global, has a significant reach and they have published two books about women leading in education. Hannah stepped down from being a strategic national leader when she became a headteacher, but it was not long before she co-founded #DiverseEd with a colleague. Hannah has recently left the system to work independently as a leadership development consultant and coach. She is the Director of Diverse Educators, delivering DE&I (Diversity, Equity and Inclusion) training to schools, trusts and teacher training institutions.

Why did you start working on the impact of gender equality in kids and why was it important for you?

I am a feminist and this influences how I show up in the world, as a human being, as an educator and as a leader. I have reflected a lot on what my parents exposed me to and did in my formative years to build my confidence and to empower me. A late 1970s baby, I was very much brought up in a home where my gender did not hold me back; where we were encouraged to make and learn from mistakes; where we were given opportunities to develop grit, character and resilience. I perhaps took this upbringing for granted until I trained to teach. I spent my first few years teaching in boys' schools and I often fell into robust conversations about gender stereotyping, gender representation and what it means to be a boy and a girl, to be male and female – with my learners, my colleagues and parents/carers. I challenged mindsets and made my students aware of things beyond their own lived experience. Moving to my first co-ed school as a middle leader, I had groups of girls who gravitated towards me, who confided in me and who positioned me as their role model. I took this responsibility seriously and recognized how I could influence, inspire and empower my students – both male and female – to be feminists.

It was when I was promoted to being a senior leader for the first time, and subsequently served as the only female on a previously all-male Senior Leadership Team in a sibling school, that my students began to openly comment on my role in challenging and changing how they saw themselves. We talked at length about glass ceilings, gendered language, inclusive behaviours and leadership styles. I realized that I had been lucky in my personal life to have visible role models, empowered women who owned their roles, their voice and their space, who I had learned to lead like through my osmosis. I actively sought female leaders in the schools and trusts I worked in who 'had it all', women who were balancing the personal and professional, but they were few and far between (where I was working anyway!). So this was what led to me co-founding a gender equality network called #WomenEd, an opportunity to connect and collaborate with women who had broken the mould and who were actively challenging the glass ceilings in our education system.

During your research and journey as an expert, what was the biggest WOW moment you had, or what was the piece of research or discovery that had the biggest impact on you?

Our first #WomenEd event made me realize the power of all female spaces. The energy in the space was electric, with 200 women wanting to be the change they wanted to see in the world. This has led to me being involved in annual International Women's Day events each March. Each year the UN publishes a different theme and we hold grassroots events where people share their stories and their journeys with each other, warts and all, so that we can learn from the collective wisdom.

I encourage my network to then pass it on to their students for Day of the Girl each year, in October. One year we created a virtual STEM toolkit to encourage girls to consider careers in this suite of subjects, which got a lot of traction across my network.

Amy Cuddy's Power Pose is a resource I use a lot in my training and talks. When I flew to Canada to launch #WomenEd Canada in April 2017, we got 2000 leaders to all do it at the same time. I regularly activated it with my whole school to boost the students' confidence for key events like exams and student council elections, and at events to empower the audience. Through my networking in the gender equality space, I got involved in LeanIn and I flew to San Francisco to join 100 global leaders who are passionate about empowering women leaders. A highlight was going to Sheryl Sandberg's house and then meeting her again when she came to London for a private breakfast event, where we discussed the need for a LeanIn book for girls too. At the LeanIn conference I experienced a D&I workshop from Google which addresses visibility and self-advocacy in the workplace. This led to me becoming an #IamRemarkable facilitator for the global Google initiative, to support under represented groups in owning and sharing their stories.

In terms of parents as principal educators, if you were to give them some practical things that they could start doing right now at home about gender stereotypes in early childhood and the effects they have on girls, what would those be?

The praise you give them:

- Focus on who they are
- Praise what they know, what they do, what they think
- Avoid praising how they look

- Affirm when they make mistakes to counter that pesky perfectionist.

The clothes you buy them:

- Challenge gender stereotyping
- Avoid pink and blue signposting for the genders
- Select empowering mottos for your girls, as well as your boys
- Avoid limiting belief statements emblazoned across their tops
- Encourage them to express themselves
- Embrace gender fluidity
- Consider trousers and leggings as being more liberating.

The roles they do:

- Expose them to everything
- Build up their skills so they can bake a cake and change a tyre
- Avoid pink and blue jobs for parents and carers
- Avoid pink and blue jobs for children.

The activities you expose them to:

- Avoid imposing limitations
- Disrupt gendered expectations of hobbies and interests
- Smash the glass ceilings with them early on
- Encourage them to get messy and dirty
- Consider what they wear – girls in leggings are more likely to go on a climbing frame.

The shows you screen:

- Consider the TV shows, films and games you expose them to
- Select shows with strong female protagonists
- Select shows written and directed by female authors
- Screen shows that challenge gender stereotypes.

The books you read:

- Review the literature you expose them to
- Select books with strong female protagonists
- Select books written by female authors
- Consider intersectional identities, i.e. race, religion, disability
- Showcase women who pioneer, challenge and disrupt the status quo.

The conversations you have:

- Teach your daughters to believe in themselves
- Teach your daughters to know their worth
- Teach your daughters to say 'no'
- Teach your daughters to have boundaries
- Teach your daughters to negotiate their worth.

The messages they receive:

- Challenge family and friends who perpetuate gender stereotypes
- Discuss unhelpful language and restrictions they receive at school
- Question things in the news and world around them
- Showcase girls who are visible role models like Malala, Rain and Greta
- Remind them that anything is possible!

For those parents wishing to learn more, are there two or three websites, books, videos, podcasts or other resources you would recommend?

This is a great question and I get asked it a lot from friends and family with daughters who are having a confidence dip. I am going to struggle to restrict it to two or three, so I'll be a rebel and give you six:

1 **Girl Guiding UK** – published a study five years ago which is still relevant research about the confidence dip or gap in girls.

There are myths to debunk about when girls lose their confidence, as there is a common misconception that it is as they transition to secondary school and/or hit puberty, but it happens a lot earlier than that.

2 **The Dove Self-Esteem project** – I originally used these resources as teacher and a tutor, but I later did some consultancy with Unilever to help the translation from US to UK contexts. In the States most schools access the body image lesson plans, worksheets and videos for parents, teachers and youth workers but it is an untapped resource in the UK.

3 *The Confidence Code for Girls* – the original book is aimed at women but this version is a self-help book aimed at girls to help them build their confidence. I bought it for my niece and she enjoyed it when she was navigating some social anxiety around friendship issues at school.

4 **Good Night Stories of Rebel Girls** – this series is brilliant for exposing girls to a range of diverse role models and female pioneers. Empowering Stories, Empowered Girls is a mission statement that really resonates with me and there is a whole website of activities for girls and their carers to explore.

5 **A Mighty Girl** – I stumbled across them via Twitter and then Facebook so I share their posts regularly with my network. As the world's largest collection of books, toys and movies for smart, confident and courageous girls, the website is a treasure trove signposting reading lists, free posters and other resources.

6 **HeForShe** – one for the dads, the step-dads, the uncles, the grandfathers, the nephews and the brothers. Lean into the campaign for gender equality, be a proud feminist and an active ally.

If you take away just a few key points from this chapter, let them be these

1 Girls don't become women in an aseptic environment in which they are truly themselves. What we refer to as 'their choices' is a mix of a lot of things.
2 We praise the looks of girls. They see us talking about other women's looks. Beauty is very soon the most important thing to aspire to for girls, and beauty is normally defined very narrowly.
3 Girls are taught to be obedient, tidy, caring, organized, not too loud, not competitive … those skills are very useful in formal education, but less so in adult life, in which women are penalized more than men for showing assertive attitudes or for setting boundaries.
4 Women are taught to be caring and empathetic. They're encouraged to pursue romantic interests as the ultimate goal and severely pushed to the path of motherhood. The definition of success for women is very different than for men.

What to do next

- Make sure they are surrounded by great role models that they can identify themselves with. It doesn't have to be within the nuclear family and it doesn't need to be just one person covering everything; there is no such a thing as the perfect role model, so the pressure is off. It is all about diversity, so make sure they are familiar with different women that have different lifestyles, skills and ideas of what being a woman is. A family friend, an auntie, a character in a book, a movie about someone. People to admire and to relate with.
- Get to know them. Without ideas and expectations. Get to admire who they are, and how they develop their personality. I find it fascinating how different my sister and I are, how different my kids are. I try to remember that some of the stereotypical things that Nora does are not because that

is 'how girls are' but because 'how Nora is' and that makes it more special.

- Let them make peace, as soon as possible, with the fact that they won't be liked by everyone and that is ok. Women that counter sexist stereotypes often pay in terms of likeability, so let's make that currency least valuable for girls. For example, if they ask you if you like something they are doing, wearing or painting, bring it back to what matters: 'Do YOU like it? The most important thing is you liking it yourself.' Or if they mention that they don't like something that you are wearing, or something in the house, or the way you are dancing, bring it back again: 'I am sorry you don't like it, but I am doing this for myself and I really like it, so it is ok.'

9

Why it matters? Boys

I spent the last chapter explaining why I find it complex and difficult to educate and parent a girl in this gendered world, but what I didn't mention is that I find it even more complex and difficult to educate and parent boys.

There is something intuitive about raising girls to be empowered, there is something natural in the pride of seeing them breaking moulds and excelling in something that the world didn't expect them to do. Pioneers in areas that society values and respects. It is almost automatic to want your daughters to avoid the things that are unfair for women, even if those things are never-ending once you start paying attention.

But what about boys? What happens when you try to parent them away from toxic masculinity, and you start to feel like you are disempowering them? What if it feels that you are failing to prepare them for a world that, like it or not, they are going to inherit? Parenting boys is more complex because part of the message we need to transmit is not as instinctive as 'you can do anything; the sky is the limit'. It's more a message about focusing on others, not taking all the space and being mindful and empathetic. It is about getting them to be pioneers of things that society doesn't value or respect that much.

As I hope is clear by now, I don't think boys are naturally any of the things that toxic masculinity normalizes in them. I think they develop those traits while navigating a world that tells them what their correct and expected way is to be. I think they are sold a complicated way to be – very celebrated, but also a cage.

I love men and boys. Even if the myth about feminists would claim otherwise. I love men and boys much more than this society does. I love them and consider them more complex than what we have been told, than what they think they are allowed to show. I love and fear men, and that is complicated, because my fear is much bigger than my love when I am coming back at night alone. I love men but also get extremely angry at them, in plural, and I am able to see a pattern in the way they treat me, or other women, and as much as I love them, also in plural, it infuriates me. I love men but I am also a bit tired of seeing them everywhere, as if the world was made by them and for them, as if it were their legitimate right to always be the main character. As much as I love men I want to see more of everyone else. I love and I grieve those men that didn't find the tools to speak up in time and found life too hard to continue. It breaks my heart because I can only imagine the solitude in the role that they have been asked to play. I love men, but it is not a straightforward love, as I have for women. It is a multi-layered and complex love that includes a lot of other feelings. And those feelings are not really about men, they are about masculinity, about what it has been defined to be and how it affects us all.

The important thing for this chapter is that even the men who represent the worst of masculinity, the ones that make it easy to lose hope with all men, they were also children once. That is why this book is very important for me, because they too were kids and we failed them, society failed them. We applauded them, laughed at their jokes, and justified them all along. We looked the other way and we said they were just being boys when they started to misbehave. We called it 'locker room conversations', while denying that there was rape culture. We spent all our time worrying about our daughters and giving them practical tips and survival techniques while we were just trusting our sons to be the good ones, as if the bad men didn't have parents that trusted them the same way. And then we justified them once again, because sure, it wasn't their fault; sure they are lovely and nice; sure it is just when they drink, or when they are out with the lads, or within the anonymity of social media. I know it is difficult to believe that our boys, our sweet boys, might be one day part of it all, but the reality is educating them for not being perpetrators is not enough, we need them to be allies and to not be enablers or bystanders.

Parenting boys is so difficult, and I find myself so over-vigilant with Eric that sometimes it makes me question myself. Am I being too harsh? Am I being more a feminist than a mum? Is this unfair, and is he is paying the price of me knowing too much? But then I think about the possible outcome if I overcompensate, and the possible outcome if I underestimate the power of toxic masculinity, and after weighing up the worst-case scenario in both situations, I make peace with how my motherhood and my feminism coexist. I know that he needs all the tools that I can give.

One of the most prevalent conversations in our family is about consent. In one way or another, we talk about consent almost daily. We talk about consent when the kids ask me to stop if I am tickling them and I make a point to note that 'look, you said stop and I have stopped'. Normally they ask for more as soon as they catch air just to ask me again to stop with their laughs inundating the room ... and I stop again and I make the exact same strong and dramatic statement with my hands up, making a really clear point about how important it is to stop if someone asks, even if they are laughing. And it continues, asking to be tickled and asking me to stop, and every single time I repeat it, 'look, I have completely stopped because you said so' and they know that it doesn't stop them asking for more.

We talk about consent when I ask them to stop putting their feet on my face when we're on the sofa, and I say it with words that they can anchor and remember, words that will keep being repeated through the weeks and years in other conversations. '*You can't do something to someone if they don't want to. Just because you want to do something and you like it, doesn't mean the other person is liking it. I am not liking this, so please stop now.'* I know my parents roll their eyes at me when they hear it, almost tempted to protect Eric, but the statistics show that a lot of men and boys haven't quite grasped those very basic rules, and I want to make sure that my kids do.

When parenting Eric I always try to keep in mind the traits that he will be encouraged to have. Sometimes he does something and I can't help but fast forward to an adult Eric in which those attitudes weren't challenged in time. I refuse to justify everything under the 'he is just 4' rule, because I have better chances now than later to set some boundaries regarding what is ok. I know it is different with Nora because she will be silenced and overcorrected, I know she won't get away with the same number of things that Eric will, I know that treating them fairly is not always treating them the same, because you have to put in the perspective that sadly we are not educating alone, that so many uninvited guests have a say regarding their upbringing – from well-intentioned family members, to teachers with different values who are set in their ways; from weird TV characters that end up being role models, to the other kids in the park who copy what they see at home and repeat it.

Nora will learn to wait her turn when speaking with others, she will learn that life is much easier when you don't take a lot of space. To be honest, if anything I am scared that Nora will learn to shrink herself to avoid being perceived as difficult. So for me it is more important that Eric learns, as soon as possible, that his opinion can't always be the most important one, that we are a family of equals and nobody is here to make his life better. That we all are the main characters in our own shows, and not just secondary characters in his. It is important for me that he learns to stand up for the things that are right, that he stays true to himself as long as possible, that he doesn't fade when someone tells him that his dress is for girls.

The boys I know are sweet and lovely, and they cry and run to their parents for hugs. And sometimes, when I see them in our laps, full of snot and tears because someone didn't share or because they really, really wanted an ice-cream and it is not fair that they couldn't have it, I wonder how many years of that we have left. How many years of unapologetic raw vulnerability, of showing their emotions and asking to be kissed better, accepting the help to navigate those emotions that seem too big.

At some stage those big emotions that once poured out of them in the shape of tears and that could disappear with the help of a hug or a kiss risk being bottled up and becoming too heavy. Although there is more work to do it is good to see that we are now talking more about the crisis in men's mental health and starting to give it the importance that it has. Death by suicide is the single biggest killer of men under 45 in the UK.[94] All the things that we ask them to carry: the pride, the pressure, the narrow definition of success, the competitiveness, the anger, the entitlement, the need for peer validation, the expectations … they are too heavy for anyone to carry alone. But we tell them that they have to.

In a study carried out by Promundo that analyses 'the man box', the name they have for the rigid norms of masculinity in young men in the UK, the USA and Mexico, we learn that 'These norms inhibit men by keeping them from expressing their true selves and from having the kind of deep connections and relationships they want. Rigid norms also affect society at large, driving inequalities, homophobia, and various forms of violence'.

The study identifies the first pillar of these rules as self-sufficiency. That understanding that they have to do it alone, that they can't ask for help, that they can't share the load. The first pillar is to leave behind the hugs or the conversations that once helped them to make peace with the big emotions and to bottle everything up instead. That is why I hold on so tightly to these moments, where I can kiss Eric and say that I am here, and that he can always tell me what is happening.

That is why every night, at dinner time, we talk about 'the best and the worst of the day', so they can normalize that we all have bad moments and that doesn't stop us from having great moments. That life is just that, a mix of the good and the bad, and the company to share it with; we share as a family, with no shame. Seeing Chris talking about being stressed, or sad, or tired, or nervous is so important for us, because one day Eric will be tempted to 'man up' and 'suck it up' which is nothing else but a recipe for resentment and anger, and the more he understands that his main role model is a complex person that is allowed all the feelings, the more he will allow himself the same.

The next pillar in that same study by Promundo is 'acting tough', defending one's reputation by using physical force if necessary. Reputation! What even is that? Do we really want our boys having to live their life with their masculinity constantly measured? Having to prove that they stick to arbitrary rules that are nothing but heritage from days that no longer represent us? Do we want them to feel that they have to live up to the standards of the sharks, and the lions, and the tigers and the boys that save the day in the TV, and the super heroes with big muscles that fight for the good with impossible weapons and violence? How is it fair that we tell them about villains and heroes who use violence to save the day, that we give them guns to play with, and surround them with predators and then call it 'nature' when they are violent?

The same report also talks about how we assume heterosexuality (and homophobia) and hypersexuality in men and, if we are honest, we know that this is true. I remember breastfeeding Eric and getting so many comments about how much he liked boobs. 'He's one of the lads'; 'His poor girlfriend, when he is older'; 'He knows what's good'; 'Bet he's in heaven with a boob always in his mouth.' It was sickening. So many friends and family members made similar jokes, of course, just for the laughs, nobody conscious of the problematic message and the awkward situation. Men are so stereotyped to be hypersexual and wear it as a badge of honour that we think that it is normal to sexualize the act of a baby feeding. I was very tempted to say the exact same things to the exact same people when it was Nora's turn to breastfeed, and to enjoy the discomfort of the moment. 'She is totally a lesbian, look how much she likes boobs!'; 'Her girlfriend will just put a boob in her mouth to shut her up if they argue' and the rest of the cringeworthy comments that were allegedly ok for Eric. Picture it for a minute. We wouldn't ever make these comments when our girl babies breastfeed and please, let's not change that! But we think it's fun, and normal, for a boy. That's all down to our concept of what being a boy and a man is, and what we encourage them to become.

It is also dangerous for them. Society's idea of men and boys being hypersexual makes it more difficult for them to report and speak about the cases in which they are the ones sexually abused. They are mocked about it, discouraged from speaking and consequently less likely to ask for help. The fact that women are the most likely victims of sexual assault doesn't erase the problem that everyone else can be too.

I don't want Eric to be a player, I don't want any of my kids to have any pressures regarding their sexual life when they grow up. I can't imagine the pressure of being a teenage boy and having to navigate such a difficult period while everyone around him is learning about sex from porn. But before we get to that stage, we need to establish the basis of the relationship we want with them so they can feel comfortable talking with us, feeling safe, and listened to, and respected. We need to normalize the act of them touching themselves (I don't mean to encourage it, simply not to shame them and to explain that it is private – and that they need to wash their hands afterwards ...), we need to have conversations about relationships and love that are grounded in respect, and about sex being pleasant, but also important and intimate. We need to create default open conversations, so we are the first people they turn to for information, instead of their also confused friends or some random videos on YouTube.

With the previous chapter, the study and the empirical evidence in mind, let's talk about John Doe this time ...

Let's imagine John leaving the hospital with his baby blue onesie, coming to a house full of baby blue and grey things and maybe some more wild and colourful items that stand up: the firemen truck pyjamas, the jungle animals, the cars. He is given some cuddly toys, and also soft balls, he is covered in cuddles and kisses, a harmless and gorgeous little one. I mean, sure, there are a couple of jokes here and there, but it's not like he can understand them, so they can't harm him, right?

He grows up in front of stories about him, about different versions of himself, of other boys. It might be the male that saves the day, that finds the solution, that fights with the monsters, that defends the town. Maybe the funny one, or the super smart one, or the shy one. As a boy, John has a variety of characters to identify with, in books and in the media, but he also has a very clear message of who is the ideal one, the aspirational one, the alpha one. It doesn't take a genius to see that some traits are more valued for the other characters, and what kind of personality gives you a higher status.

He is encouraged to play with toys that reinforce his spatial skills, and he is brought outside to explore his wilderness, he is given a ball, and a bike, and a scooter, celebrated for being fast and encouraged to get up and keep going if he falls. 'It's nothing, come on, get back on.' He notices very quickly that the adults don't celebrate him that much when he plays with the pink things or the kitchen, even if they are fun. He notices that the other boys don't do it, that in the catalogue there are only girls playing with that toy. And he gets very soon that there is an 'us' and there is a 'them'. That boys are boys and girls are girls. And that they are split in different lines in the queue in school – just for ease – and that they are wearing different uniforms, and that they have different hair-styles and play with different things, are praised for different things and there are things that are ok for one but not for the other. He knows that every time there is trouble everyone expects him to be causing it, especially if he is in a group with other boys; he also knows that although he is told off more often, it is also less severely.

He knows that he doesn't want to cry like a girl, whatever that means. He knows that being perceived as a girl is wrong, and he soon exaggerates how much he doesn't like something that looks slightly feminine. He knows that big boys don't do this or that other thing. People touch his muscles and pretend to be amazed about how super strong he is, they tell him he is the fastest when he runs, the one that jumped the highest, the best player on the field … everyone lets him win, but he doesn't know that yet, he craves that attention and validation and he becomes a sore loser, because nobody ever taught him to lose with grace, to win with grace. If he likes a sport he is suddenly expected to excel and make it big, parents shouting at referees at school matches. I know this happens with girls, too, but it happens less. And John hears his masculine role models screaming at the TV during a match, he's given a football shirt and expected to be loyal to the team, and to feel a sense of belonging. Of brotherhood.

Adolescence for John is not a walk in the park. Hormones, smells, knowing nothing, feeling everything, immense peer pressure, a lack of diverse role models with different interpretations of success, being bombarded by toxic masculine figures: in videogames, in films, in books, etc. John knows that popularity is basically liking sports, and being liked by girls. There are other options, of course, but they are also stereotyped and who really wants to be the nerd, considering how they are presented in the media? (Don't get me wrong, I still think it is easier to be a boy nerd than a girl nerd, but I don't think any such role models are great when you are a teenager.) There is so much toxic masculinity around John, at a stage where he is the most vulnerable and lost, he might even fall down a rabbit hole into the alt right groups that target and groom boys like John. As Laura Bates explains in her book *Men Who Hate Women*, they use boys' vulnerability and convert it to rage, they target them and follow them where they hang out (online in games, in gyms, reading sport pages). In the period where John needs the most answers and hand holding, he is the most ridiculed when he asks for help and opens up to his peers. He is becoming, and expected to be, a man, and whatever that looks for him will change everything. But let's be honest, a lot of the things that will get decided have been reinforced for years, from the beginning, and there is so much that we can do, up to this point, to hold more control.

John wants to be bulked, he wants a six pack and toned arms. He wants to be tall (what a currency for men!) and maintain his hair as much as possible, the masculine jaw, he wants to 'be able to grow a beard'. He is surrounded by comments and jokes about how the masculinity is measured in centimetres in your pants, the bigger the better, more masculine, more desired. Sadly, we are not becoming more open-minded about how women should look, what we are doing is making men fall into the traps of physical tyranny. Yes, it might not be as cruel and strict as it is with women, at least yet, but it doesn't mean that is not a problem and definitely this is not the right way to achieve equality.

It is difficult for John, as a man, especially as a young man or older boy, to navigate and hear about feminism. When you are so used to privilege, equality feels like oppression. Why are we talking about that again? Why do women have International Women's Day? And month!? Why are there suddenly all these books and films that are about women in history – how is that fair?

It is the small things that John has always seen and on which nobody has challenged him or invited him to reconsider more critically. Sure, we watch men's football because it is better; sure, we talk about men's sport because it's better; only a few years ago there were more men called John than women CEOs of big companies but sure, that must be because men are better at business.[95] John thinks that women like to be beautiful; they want to marry, they want to be given presents, and to be taken out for dinner, and to be spoilt. If he stopped to think about it he would see how, in that version, women live their lives in the passive voice, where things are done for them, and to them.

John is supposed to want as many girls as possible, but if he decides to settle down it has to be with one like those in the films that he watches, the woman that is basically a man but also hot, the one that is not like other women. But also, the one that is wife-material, the one that you wouldn't be ashamed to introduce to your parents and co-workers and friends. Hot but not too hot, sexy but in a respectable way (as if there were another way), smart but not too smart, funny – but not more than him. Because normal women talk too much, and are shallow, they are always nagging their partners, they never cut men any slack. If you ask John, he will tell you that he loves women, but how much about womanhood does he know? How much do men really know about women, about their bodies, their minds, their hopes? We don't encourage them to grow up together, we don't talk with normality about simple things like periods and clitoral pleasure, or about hormone changes, or mental load. Men are not given the chance to understand and love womanhood, because womanhood is a deviation from the 'normal', it is niche.

It is really important to stress here how intersectionality is also at play for boys. We can't really understand masculinity without at least mentioning the nuances of power for different boys and men from differing socioeconomic/class and racial/cultural backgrounds. For some boys, who become men, certain aspects of masculinity are not only mandatory and omnipresent within their role models, but it is also a matter of safety.

So, here is adult John and *please note that in my example John is white, to make a stronger point about holding all the privilege, most times not being aware of it. Obviously other intersections will make John's story different.* Our John, the little child that cried for mummy in the park and was so harmless in his baby blue onesies. He is a big businessperson now, very serious with a big salary, closing deals and feeling that he deserves everything because he had to work for every single thing: he hates the word privilege because nobody gave him anything for free. And that's true, he worked to get there, but was the field the same? Did he have the same obstacles along the way as his that were not men? Was he given extra burdens, extra expectations, extra demands and extra loads with which to compete? Has he stopped to think that it is not about what he had to do to get there, it's about what others would have had to do to get to the same place? Has he asked himself: why? Has anyone taught him to ask himself: why?

The journey behind those differences starts at the very beginning, from that 20-week scan. From those kicks in the belly that are received with the hope of a footballer in the making or with jokes about the temperamental daughter that you are going to have to deal with. And it is our job to correct as much as we can, and also to explain the things that we can't, and to hold their hands and show them differently.

No, men are not simple, or predators, or poorer carers. They are just taught to be, and then excused for being so, like it's part of their nature. We need to see fathers shown as the main carers in TV shows, men talking about mental health in films, men at the top of businesses speaking up for their female colleagues, cool guys stopping the sexist comments. We need to redefine masculinity, so it is something freeing for them and for the rest.

I don't want to scare you, and I know you will look at the kids you know and you will refuse to believe that they will become any of the things that I talk about. I know you do because I do, too, when I look at Eric. Educating a son is the biggest responsibility but it is also an amazing opportunity to redefine with them, hand in hand and from the beginning, what being a man is for this new generation, and to do it proudly.

Expert interview: Owen Thomas

Owen Thomas is the Head of Programmes (Fathers) at Future Men. He has over 15 years' extensive direct experience working closely with fathers and male carers at crucial stages of their lives. He has responsibility supervising a team of fathers at work – project co-ordinators across London, offering direct support and interventions to fathers, young fathers and young men, including having oversight of the Future Dads expectant fathers' programme.

An element of this role is strategic – advocating for the needs of young and expectant fathers at local and national forums such as the All-Party Parliamentary Group on Fatherhood, and delivering training and workforce development to professionals. This also includes consultation on a broad range of related subjects, such as addressing stereotypes of masculinities, culture and identity, healthy relationships, teenage pregnancy and preventative work.

This work at Future Men has informed research/policy across a wide range of issues, especially around marginalized and disadvantaged boys and young men's needs, their families, and how this affects the wider community.

Why did you start working with boys and men and how have they been affected by a narrow definition of masculinity? Why was it important for you?

I started working with boys and men as an extension to wider youth/play and community work I got involved in as a young man and father trying to find rewarding work that drew on my life experiences.

I had tried different kind of jobs (from office work to media to more manual jobs), needing to find regular paid work to support myself and my daughter. I felt the chance to work with children and young people was great, especially at the time when the UK still invested in youth and play work, and aligned with my pre-existing value set instilled in me by my parents: a core interest in fairness, equity, justice and fair play.

The aforementioned skill set, along with a first-hand understanding of being from a marginalized group (being of mixed race) growing up in Thatcher's Britain in a highly demonized and deprived area (Brixton), meant that I had a clear sense of how working with young people could help bring individual changes as well as empowering people to achieve wider social and community changes for the better. Therefore, when the chance to work for a charity supporting young fathers in a South London borough arose, it helped me see that what was a life-defining factor for me (fatherhood) could be utilized to bring about positive outcomes for other young men. In supporting them to be the best dads they could be, they could also take from the experience the chance to grow and re-evaluate some of the narrow lanes we had been given to operate in, in order to get more from life.

Growing up working class, from an ethnic minority and socially excluded from many opportunities, meant that during my formative years there were many competing value systems at play: the values instilled by family and community vs. the values instilled by wider society of that era – individualism, patriarchy, rampant capitalism. For me and a lot of my peers, all this coalesced into a torrid soup which led to many risky and challenging experiences which I was lucky to steer myself through relatively unscathed and still in possession of my liberty. This did not exist in isolation, there was always a wider sense of a greater community spirit than exists now, a focus on communal action and a fight for equality across many areas of life, which also compete to be primary in my life.

Then fatherhood arrived and helped me to fall back on the core values and realize that here was a piece of me outside of my physical form that needed care and nurturing; I needed to make decisions fairly swiftly on what my wider life priorities should be. Luckily my support networks helped me realize that being a hands-on father and playing an active role in the care and upbringing of my child was paramount to me. Having a daughter also redoubled my commitment to fairness and understanding the nuances of life and the interchange between the sexes – we need each other.

The old systems put in place to keep society ordered had clearly not been set up to aid me (as a non-white man) and similarly had not been set up to help the majority of women. Moving away from harmful stereotypes about everyone seemed a logical progression. I wanted to set an example to my child of fairness and understanding, and I wanted her to be free. This encouraged a more open approach to my role as a man, as well as sharing with my peers how rewarding this was on many levels – as a father, partner and human being not being beholden to the negative frameworks of masculinity whilst retaining a strong sense of self and identity. None of it is easy, but it is right.

Most boys and men that I and my organization support have some sense of this and, with help, have moved themselves to positions that are more open – they are able to break from the norms that restrict them and others around them. This is not a done deal by any means – in the last five to ten years I have noticed significant backwards steps in equality of the sexes alongside wider injustices in society. When pressure hits it is much harder to pursue wider social justice goals and to help those struggling to focus on higher ideals.

When the day-to-day struggle is more pronounced it can be dangerous for many to break away from the mould of what men should do, as conforming to it brings a degree of security in an often insecure or dangerous, intolerant world.

However, I believe in continuing to work the way we do – with a focus on positive masculinity – we help those we work with and wider society.

During your journey and your experience on the ground, what was the biggest WOW moment you had, or what was the piece of research that had the biggest impact on you?

I have had many WOW moments over the years I have been doing this kind of work, repeated moments of realization with men, particularly young men, from marginalized communities. Those who have often been written off and who have been conditioned to hold strongly negative views but have been flexible enough to shift those views and begin to be curious about some of the reasons why society is the way it is, and how it impacts why they are the way they are.

It is always impressive to see someone who has been labelled as dangerous and feckless step up and adapt to their new role and responsibilities, take positive steps towards accepting responsibility. It is really rewarding seeing them not only fit the provider role as a father (an acceptable male dynamic) but become a hands-on caregiver, doing school runs, changing nappies, owning domestic duties, being sensitive and showing vulnerability. It is great the way they change and adapt to new problem solving and conflict resolution methods – and how they give up some of the meagre power they have (through violence or anger) and take the often risky step of letting this be replaced by calm consideration and thoughtful actions. This is always a massive WOW moment for me.

In terms of research there have been many great studies that begin to highlight these journeys, including the Following Young Fathers research by Leeds Trinity University and the Following Young Fathers further research. Dr Brid Featherstone has done some amazing research into gender roles and how they affect familial outcomes.

In terms of parents as principal educators, if you were to give them two or three practical things that they could start doing right now at home about giving specifically boys a better chance to not be defined by stereotypes, what would those be?

Modelling behaviour is key; give examples of being flexible and open to doing things outside of the norm or expected behaviours. Children are very driven by wider outside factors and pressures so parents showing by example that Dad does the dishes and Mum likes sport are small but important first steps.

Reading is key for boys, this leads to a curiosity about the world around you and the beginnings of retaining knowledge. This should be encouraged even if it doesn't seem to be an initial interest; comics are great to get started.

For those parents wishing to learn more, are there any particular websites, books, videos, podcasts or other resources you would recommend to help them?

The Fawcett Society's recent report on gender stereotypes in the early years has great examples of practical tips for parents, educators and wider society on how to challenge harmful stereotypes.

I have recently participated in an online symposium hosted by Men Engage, an international coalition of organizations working with men and boys to tackle gender inequality. This event, called Ubuntu, has garnered a broad range of sessions, discussions, resources and presentations, many of which are captured online. I recommend checking some of that content out.

The Open University has done some great work over the years collating and partnering with other academic institutions to create reports like Beyond Male Role Models, which give a nuanced take on gender stereotypes.

My own organization <www.Futuremen.org> has a range of resources available to support parents.

If you take away just a few key points from this chapter, let them be these

1 Boys don't inherit toxic masculinity, but instead develop these traits and habits when they are taught by society the stereotyped view of how they should be portrayed.
2 Boys, outward appearance is also held to a high standard (tall, strong, masculine features). We seem to be aiming for 'equality' by creating a cross-gender tyranny.
3 It is very difficult for boys and men (especially if white, middle class, heterosexual ...) to understand their own privilege because they have always seen themselves represented in society and they hold the majority of the space, voices and power and it can be taken for granted.
4 We can't have equality without men being on board with it. And that means to not only support women, but also to embrace a broader idea of masculinity that doesn't exist as an opposition of what is perceived as feminine.

What to do next

- Same here as for everyone else! Make sure they are surrounded by great role models that they can identify with. Let them see men that cry, that care, that understand success in a different way than the expected one. Let them engage and see as much diversity as possible regarding what the new masculinity is.
- No surprises here either. Get to know them, without ideas and expectations. Get to admire who they are, and how they develop their personality. See the things that they do, what they like and enjoy as something personal, not as something 'typical' or 'atypical'. We are all the mix of all the typical and atypical things that make us unique.

- Make sure they understand consent. That is important for everyone, but mostly for boys, no need to lie here. Make sure they understand that no means no, that stop means stop and that something is only fun if everyone is having fun. Make sure they understand they are not being wronged if someone politely says that they don't like something, or that they don't want to play at that game.
- Celebrate the things that are not typical, in him and in other boys and men. Verbally mention how much you admire his availability to tell you his feelings and how important it is that he feels comfortable crying and recognizing his sadness. Tell him how good someone looks in those (counter-stereotypical) clothes. How fun that (counter-stereotypical) activity they are doing seems. How cool it is that they like this (counter-stereotypical) thing. The pressure they have to put things into boxes is immense, it is good to get them out of there every so often.

10

Why it matters? Trans kids

During the previous chapters of the book I have been speaking about my children as a boy and a girl, and so far this is what I know them as – they refer to themselves as 'boy' and 'girl' and are consistent about it, whether they are dressed up as a princess or as Spider-Man.

If you are wondering whether I would be worried about either of them being non-binary, the answer is of, course, yes. I would be worried about not being able to help them as much as I would want to, I would be scared of falling short while navigating things and adding to a complex situation, I would be worried about them having to suffer because society is still transphobic, I would be worried about the rejection they might endure because people are scared of what feels different. But if they are non-binary, I want them to live their life as such, I don't want them to compromise and suffocate their identity just out of fear. I want them to make the most of who they are, not of what the world tells them that they are. I would be worried about all of us failing them, and not for a second the other way round.

I am not worried or scared about my kids, or any kids, exploring gender in a much broader and freer way than we did. Actually, I know a lot of adults who are only now making peace with the fact that 'woman' or 'man' is not quite how they identify and I love that for them! You can be a very masculine woman and identify as a woman, you can be a very feminine-presenting female and still not quite feel like a woman, you are allowed to search for the identity that makes you feel at home no matter how you look. Aesthetics and identity, although a lot of time related because both express how we present to the world, can have different journeys.

I talk a lot about the trans and non-binary community with my mother, who is very respectful and eager to learn but just doesn't fully 'get it'. It makes me laugh because it is almost as if she feels like it is an exam, one that she is really keen to pass because she knows it's important. She will ask me things like, 'but are there people that don't have gender at all?' or 'do we use the same name for people that have had an operation as for people that have not? Surely if you have had an operation then you can't be non-binary because you are a gender from the binomial?'. 'So, I am cisgender, right? That means being the same gender as the one I was expected to be at birth?' She often apologises, saying that although she respects it and she will call anyone whatever she is told, she feels unable to learn all the details and ramifications. And that's ok; I mean, she's in her sixties, and much more forward thinking than many of my fellow millennials, definitely more than most of her generation. Non-binary people are shaking up the world as we know it, and sometimes just accepting that you won't fully understand it, but still addressing it with humility, kindness and respect, is enough.

The way I see it, normalizing gender as a spectrum is the ultimate step to dismantling a lot of the injustices based on gender. Some people within some sections of feminism argue the opposite, that we should abolish gender all together, that if nobody had gender and we just stuck to sex (female/male) based on our genitalia that would be the end of the problem. They also feel that a lot of injustices are sex-related and by including trans women in the feminist cause, we are watering the injustices caused by sex.

I disagree. I think that we sadly have a lot of work to do, in both sex and gender areas, and even if we can't give our energy to all in the same way, we can definitely acknowledge them all.

Of course we can't fight equally every single cause in the world because our energy is limited but if, instead of fighting about who deserves to benefit from our activism and who doesn't and having a message of hate, we rechannelled all that time and effort to fight the medical data gap, rape culture, gender violence or genital mutilation, we would move faster towards our common goal. Excluding people from our cause shouldn't ever be our priority, we have urgent things to do.

The day that we can fully accept that gender is a spectrum, we will all win. But it might start by also admitting that sex is a spectrum too, giving up completely the idea of two only opposite sexes and embracing instead the bimodal with plenty of intersections. I will recommend to you, at the end of the chapter, some science-based books that corroborate that. Unlearning and letting go the comfort of the simplicity, the repeated, the assumed is the first step.

For me, winning looks like letting go of assumptions and stereotypes about what a person is, and instead showing a genuine interest in who a person is. Welcoming everyone in the world with no expectations about their gender and celebrating their uniqueness without loading them up with baggage. To me that is what the future looks like. Or should.

Imagine. We wouldn't have the same level of discrimination because we wouldn't assume anything just for the way a person is dressed, or their name, or their pronouns. Not only would the non-binary community be better off, but everybody else would benefit, too. What is not to love about everyone having the space and freedom to explore one's true self away from any kind of gender dictatorship? What is wrong with all of us having the ability to tune in with the way we like to be referenced, to have a say in how we want society to refer to us.

Even in 2021 it still takes a lot of bravery for non-binary people to fully accept who they are and live their life accordingly, and that sucks. Nobody should be 'inspirational' or 'brave' for living their life in a way that is theirs, and theirs only. I bet non-binary people would change their inspirational status for consistent respect. I know I would.

Kids are watching, and learning, and they are figuring themselves out and figuring the world out every day. They pick up the rules (spoken or unspoken) and they very quickly understand what is apparently ok and what is discouraged. Not every child is willing to push as hard to explore outside the box that they are given, and not every family builds those boxes with the same space or flexibility. For some of the kids it will be less challenging, for others it will be the beginning of a lifetime of internalized conflict.

I am not trained in this topic, but I am constantly learning and reading about it because it is one of the biggest of our time. The same way that sexual orientation was one of the biggest topics for the generation before us. Because let's not forget that we were having these conversations about sexual orientation not that long ago, even if for most of us it is now a no brainer.

We now know that sexuality is a spectrum, we all know gay people, bisexual people, asexual people ... we are less afraid to talk about those topics and we are starting to see some representation around us. I am not saying the battle is over, we are still a severely homophobic society; we still assume that every child is going to be heterosexual and we speak to them as such. We operate as if everyone is straight unless proven otherwise, which consequently passes the load of correction (which includes awkwardness in the best case scenario, and fear in the worst) to the people that already have had it tougher.

When people say that we have more gay people now than ever, what they are saying, even if they don't know it, is 'we have freed a lot of people and they can now live their best life, outside outdated concepts that didn't represent them'. Of course, there are more (openly) gay people in countries where there is space to be so. Of course, people that would have never allowed themselves to question their sexual orientation now may do so. Of course, the vocabulary, the role models and the representation invite us all to listen to ourselves and to get to know ourselves better instead of living with the inertia of the norm. But isn't that positive? A society full of repressed heterosexual-presenting people isn't any healthier than a society in which everyone is given full autonomy to move across a whole spectrum. A life in which you are allowed to like everyone, to fall in love with everyone.

The history of left-handedness

Rate of left-handedness among Americans, by year of birth

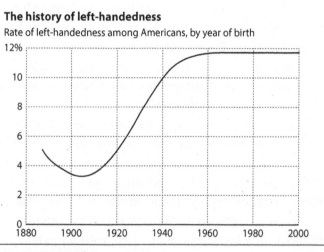

WAPO.ST/**WONKBLOG**
Source: Survey data reported in 'The History and Geography of Human Handedness' (2009)

This graph shows the 'raise' of left-handed people, in the early/mid 1900s, when it started to be socially accepted and children weren't punished for it at school. It then plateaued at a steady rate.[96]

I think most of us in this generation are more open to queerness regarding sexual orientation, even if we still hold learnt discriminatory unconscious attitudes. We still talk about mothers and fathers, we still ask people about their boyfriends, girlfriends, husbands or wives. We still make so many assumptions and force gay people to effectively 'come out' daily, to strangers, to receptionists in hotels, to the teacher in nursery, to the other parents in the park. Being gay is still exhausting and not as easy as being the perceived human neutral, heterosexual. So, don't get me wrong, we still have work to do, but at least gay people are no longer constantly described as 'brave' or 'inspirational' for just existing.

We get in our heads that idea (when not fear) of our kids being gay from the very early stages, at moments where kids are not sexually or romantically attracted to anyone yet. The first important thing is to stop sexualizing kids, they are not sexual beings yet. They feel pleasure if they touch themselves because touching yourself is pleasant, but it is not sexual, not in the way adults understand sex. There is no natural shame about touching themselves unless we create it, there is nothing perverted about finding out why or how their genitalia are different than others unless we see it through our adult lenses, and there is nothing lustful in kids learning about bodies, including the way bodies feel.

It doesn't mean that we shouldn't acknowledge and respect kids' capacity for romantic interest, or crushes, in childhood. Without any doubt we should respect them and not try to 'correct' them, mock them or devalue them. Maybe ask some questions and use it as an opportunity to show that you are listening, that you care about their life, that you are there without judging.

But most kids, especially in those early ages, don't want or care about girlfriends or boyfriends really, they are just playing with other kids, and imitating/role playing what they see at home or in films (which are too focused on romantic love from too early on, especially the ones catered to girls). Nora and Eric want to marry each other and every time I tell them that they won't be able to marry because they are siblings they say 'not now! When we are older!' as if the limitation was their age, as with drinking coffee or staying up late. I use this to bring to their level the different concepts of fraternal vs. romantic love, and still celebrate that they love each other and want to spend time together forever. 'If you ever have a partner that you want to marry, it will be outside your family, but you are always going to be siblings and love each other.' I don't want to make marriage a given, and I want them to be used to the word 'partner'. A lot of the small conversations are useful for planting seeds.

We can stop normalizing boy meets girl, they date, they marry, they have kids, they pass the same stereotypical expectations to their children and they die. We can open a whole world of options for them, including a childfree life, a non-married life, a single life, etc. We can stop adding moral value to lifestyle choices and just present them honestly, with their pros and their cons, so when our kids make choices throughout their lives we can be proud that those choices were real, free and informed. Even if they are not the ones that we would have made for them.

While opening up all the options (career choices, hobbies, civil state) we should also open up a whole world of realities in terms of gender. Not only opening up what being a woman or being a man is (which is very important!) but also to celebrate and bring visibility to everything else. Because it exists, because it is not going anywhere (and why should it?) and because the sooner we come to peace with it, the easier we will make it for the ones to come.

I don't know if any of my kids are going to come out as non-binary at some point, I have no way of knowing that, but I would be really surprised if neither one of them, or all the friends that I will meet through their lives, didn't turn out to be. I will be surprised if in this generation both my children and every single child that we have a friendly relationship with just happens to be strict on their cisgender identity. As the adult part of their life, even if not as parents, we have a responsibility to children and, more importantly, we should have a willingness to be a positive influence in their lives. I want every kid to feel that the world is a safe space, but because that is definitely out of my scope, I am committed to make my home a safe space for everyone. A space where there are no things for boys or for girls, in which we educate with kindness and respect about the complexity of gender, a home in which we go out of our way to have diverse books and references so they can absorb and ask questions. I want my house to be the place where pronouns are respected, bigotry is not allowed, and curiosity is normal and celebrated. Not only for Eric and Nora, but for every child that crosses our threshold.

Of course, kids will have questions. My mum has questions; I have questions; obviously kids, who have questions about literally everything, will have questions! From birth, they have been divided into two very clear societal groups and, of course, it is confusing to be presented with the idea that there are more groups out there, but their curiosity is harmless, and it is beautiful, and it is the best conversation starter.

I was showing them a video of Jeffrey Marshall, a non-binary author and activist, singing the other day and they were fascinated by them. 'Mum, it is a boy, but it is also a girl!' We talked about how some people were both things, or neither, and that some people look like Jeffrey but they are women, some others look like Jeffrey but they are boys, and some others are non-binary. There was excitement in their confusion and the feeling that they will understand more in the future. Kids are very intuitive, they know that they don't understand everything, they know that they can't do everything just yet, and they are ok with it, as long as they know that they can come to us to help them understand what they can.

It is up to us whether we hide it under the carpet ('don't stare, it is rude') or include it as something else in our children's lives, the same way we talk about diversity of religions even if we only believe in one, or none; the same way we talk and educate about the diversity of races, or body shapes, or physical abilities. We just need to keep in mind that they will eventually find out, that they will have to deal with this topic, that some of our kids will be non-binary and most of them will have friends that are. How they live all those events starts in the early years.

I want to go through a very overall idea of what it looks like for Jo Doe, but it is very broad because non-binary is an extremely complex umbrella that covers different identities. The experience of a trans kid with gender dysphoria who ends up having surgery is not the same as the reality of a gender-fluid person who doesn't experience dysphoria, to mention two cases in point. But let's put down a sample view of things that they could have in common.

Jo is brought home in their very gendered coloured onesie and treated stereotypically. Their parents, family and friends can't help but believe what they've been told, that kids with those genitalia like certain things, and act in certain ways.

Jo starts to feel confronted every time they do things differently than expected, they notice jokes around them, sometimes subtle and sometimes abrupt corrections of what they should be liking or how they should be acting. The other kids feel that Jo is defying the rules and they make jokes, too, especially those who haven't been educated around diversity, especially kids with severe rules about gender at home. Those kids in the park make fun of Jo, they police the way they play and what they choose. Jo is brave enough to push through and stay true to what they want to do, but it hurts, and it makes them question themselves. It seems that the other kids have it easier. If only Jo could be just like others.

That goes on and on. Jo's parents are worried and feel that, in order to save their child from a life of discrimination, they need to try even harder to make them realize that they are wrong, that it's a phase, that they should stop seeking attention and just be *normal*. They repeat the world 'normal' as if Jo's own existence were an abnormality, a wrongness ... and Jo starts to wonder if they are right. The isolation from peers also goes on – being non-binary doesn't rank high in the popularity metrics. By the time romantic and sexual interest arrive in Jo's life they are even more lost than their peers. In their teenage years, in which it is already hard enough to navigate hormones, social life and school for everyone, Jo has the extra burden of not finding enough role models, not fully identifying with the stories that they have always been told. Jo is more vulnerable in a time where they all are going through a lot. We should note here that a recent large study within the LGBTQ+ community found that 60 per cent of trans and non-binary youths had engaged in self harm, and 50 per cent reported having seriously considered suicide.[97]

A lot of day-to-day things are just more difficult for Jo. Filling in forms, going to the doctor, dating, going shopping, interviewing for jobs. Sometimes they just want to be Jo the professional person, or the nice neighbour, or the invisible citizen on the bus, but people have difficulty seeing behind the non-binary part of them. They are non-binary, of course, but they are much more than that.

And to make things more difficult there are all the debates, constantly, about their existence. People who have never experienced what Jo has are jumping into the discussion to loudly voice their own opinions, telling people like Jo to compromise, as if Jo hadn't been compromising, in the best-case scenario, all their life. People expect Jo to give up their right to use the correct bathroom, people claim that they find it a hassle to learn their pronouns, people keep saying that this is a psychiatric issue. Jo is accused of trying to steal rights from other collectives, even if the historical social advancements are full of people like Jo. They don't have the choice to not be an activist because their whole existence is a challenge to a system, being themselves is an act of revolution. An exhausting one.

I don't know if Eric or Nora are going to have to go through any of that, but we don't have to live it in person in this family in order to educate ourselves and be allies. We don't need to change the world only for our kids when the time arrives, we can also do it for Jo. We can proactively educate our kids about this reality, and make sure they are kind and respectful and open minded with the other kids, or adults. We can normalize it from the earliest years so whatever happens our kids will be part of the solution, and not part of the problem.

Extra resource: A quick and simplified guide to get us started

I did this guide with the resources of genderspectrum.org,[98] Georgie Williams and an article from Laurel Wamsley[99]

Sex

Male/female assignation at birth, this term refers to a person's external genitalia, hormonal levels, chromosomes and internal reproductive organs. When a person is assigned a particular sex at birth, it is often mistakenly assumed that this will equate with their gender; it might, but it might not.

Intersex is not a gender identity, it describes someone born with anatomical, hormonal and/or chromosomal variations in their sex characteristics. Some intersex people self-define as trans and/or non-binary, others with the gender they were assigned at birth.

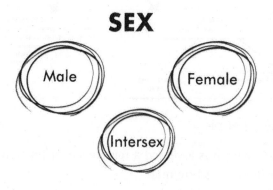

Gender

Our body, identity and social gender (how we present our gender in the world and how individuals, society, culture and community perceive, interact with and try to shape our gender) are three distinct, but interrelated, components that comprise a person's experience of gender. Each of these dimensions can vary greatly across a range of possibilities. A person's comfort in their gender is related to the degree to which these three dimensions feel in congruence.

It is much more complex than sex, and we can primarily divide people into two groups:

1. **Cisgender/Cis**: someone whose gender identity aligns with the gender they were assigned at birth (cis- from Latin, meaning 'on this side [of]', in contrast to trans, from the Latin root meaning 'across', 'beyond' or 'on the opposite side [of]').
2. **Trans**: a gender identity and umbrella term for people whose gender differs from, or does not sit comfortably within, the gender assigned at birth based on their sex. Within the trans umbrella there are people that have a gender identity that is binary and people that have a gender identity that is non-binary.

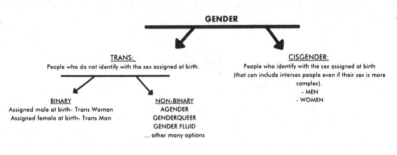

Trans binary people

- A person who was assigned a female sex at birth and whose gender identity is boy/man.
- A person who was assigned a male sex at birth and whose gender identity is girl/woman.

Within this group there are people that decide to bring themselves and/or their bodies into alignment with their gender identity. Transitioning can include **any, none** or **all** of the following. It is important to know that what any person does to be aligned is completely personal.

- **Social congruence measures**: changes of social identifiers such as clothing, hairstyle, gender identity, name and/or pronouns.
- **Hormonal congruence measures**: the use of medical approaches such as hormone 'blockers' or hormone therapy to promote physical, mental and/or emotional alignment.
- **Surgical congruence measures**: the addition, removal or modification of gender-related physical traits.
- **Legal congruence measures**: changing identification documents such as one's birth certificate, driver's licence or passport.

Gender dysphoria refers to psychological distress that results from an incongruence between one's sex assigned at birth and one's gender identity. Not all trans people experience dysphoria, and those who do may experience it at varying levels of intensity. Gender dysphoria is a diagnosis listed in the *Diagnostic and Statistical Manual of Mental Disorders*. Some argue that such a diagnosis inappropriately pathologizes gender incongruence, while others contend that a diagnosis makes it easier for transgender people to access necessary medical treatment.

Trans non-binary people

A gender identity and an umbrella term for people whose identity falls outside the gender binary. Some people do not identify wholly or at all with the gender they were assigned at birth – some people have no gender at all. The term non-binary comes under the trans umbrella.

- **Agender:** a person who sees themselves as not having a gender. Some agender-identified people see themselves as being gender neutral rather than not having any gender but, in any case, do not identify with a gender.

- **Genderfluid:** people who have a gender or genders that change. Genderfluid people move between genders, experiencing their gender as something dynamic and changing, rather than static.
- **Genderqueer:** an umbrella term (under the trans umbrella) to describe someone who doesn't identify with conventional gender identities, roles, expressions and/or expectations. For some, genderqueer is a non-binary identification, and for others it is not.
- Many more options ...

Sexual orientation

Our sexual orientation and our gender are separate, though related, parts of our overall identity. Gender is personal (how we each see ourselves), while sexual orientation is interpersonal (who we are physically, emotionally and/or romantically attracted to).

Expert interview: Georgie Williams

Georgie Williams is a professional gender and sexuality consultant, and a graduate of the MSc Gender programme at the London School of Economics and Political Science. They specialize in transgender, genderqueer, non-binary and intersex research and education, and founded the /Queer project in 2018 – a global platform for gender and sexuality research and resources. /Queer is also a Kinsey Institute archived podcast used in university curricula, both in the UK and USA. Georgie lectures and researches from their standpoint as a non-binary transgender individual.

Why did you start working on queer research and divulgation and why was it important for you?

I started researching queer (gender and/or sexuality variant) culture and issues during my undergraduate studies in 2015, but I have been personally invested since my own coming out about my sexuality at 15 years old, in 2010. When my coming out irreversibly shattered my relationship with my mother, the grief that emerged eventually evolved into a sense of motivation – I wanted to help ensure that 20, 30 years down the line, it is unthinkable within our culture to disown a child over their gender and sexuality. Since I started my professional engagement in queer research and activism I have watched the focus of the movement shift ever closer towards trans inclusivity and, as someone who is non-binary (and thus identifies under the umbrella of transgender), this is highly encouraging. The social movement and the consequential research no longer exclusively focuses on sexuality as it feels like it did even just five years ago.

During your journey and your experience on the ground, what was the biggest WOW moment you had, or what was the piece of research that had the biggest impact on you?

It is hard to pin down one specific moment but, back in 2017 when I was undertaking my masters degree in Gender in London, I read a fantastic article about a prominent Waria activist (Waria is a third gender in Indonesia, the closest 'western' equivalent is a transgender woman). Waria have had to fight tirelessly for their rights against a wave of Indonesian conservatism that incorrectly postulates that Waria are 'LGBT' – western and modern – instead of a traditional facet of Indonesian culture, which they historically are. I read this article about the activist Shinta Ratri with fervour and, three years later, was completely knocked sideways to walk into a meeting at an NGO in Indonesia about my upcoming research exhibition and find Ibu (Madam) Shinta sitting at the table, putting herself forward as a collaborator for my exhibition. It was a real full-circle moment for me and a huge honour.

In terms of parents as principal educators, if you were to give them two or three practical things that they could start doing, right now at home, about giving specifically non-binary kids a better chance to not be defined by stereotypes, what would those be?

Firstly, *allow a dialogue.* Just because your child has had less time on the planet than you have doesn't mean they don't have a better idea of their internal feelings about themselves than you do. This is not to say that children are an authority when it comes to gender identity! Merely that gender is something we all personally experience. Let them vocalize how they feel about their body and their identity without shame or judgement – these feelings may or may not change over time, but this is not unusual. Gender, after all, is no more a static concept than any other part of the human psyche and may change and develop over time. Empathy is the most effective tool in your arsenal.

Secondly, *facilitate experimentation.* Most non-binary children will want to explore their outward presentation – this is entirely harmless, since clothes and hairstyles are not innately gendered. Beyond allowing a child to explore their identity, this also cements a sense of trust in you as their parent. Ultimately, non-binary children just want someone to be fighting their corner with them.

Thirdly, *affirm your child's feelings and thoughts.* Some of us really do go without unconditional love from our parents and your non-binary child may fear losing you as a consequence of their identity. At the end of the day, your child hasn't changed, they've emerged. Go that extra mile to reassure them that you don't love them any less for being who they are.

For those parents wishing to learn more, are there any particular websites, books, videos, podcasts or other resources you would recommend to help them?

I cannot recommend Mermaids enough as a service for parents of transgender and/or non-binary youths. I had the honour and pleasure of volunteering with them for three years and their helpline, webchat and forums make a world of difference to trans children and their parents. If you want to further understand how pervasive and ultimately normal being transgender is, I recommend *Transgender History* by Susan Stryker. If you wish to learn more about the experiences of trans young people, I also recommend *Beyond Magenta: Transgender Teens Speak Out* by Susan Kuklin. In terms of specific non-binary information, follow everything the wonderful Fox and Owl Fisher do. As a non-binary couple whose trailblazing activism has changed the political and cultural landscape in the UK for non-binary people, I cannot sing their praises enough.

If you take away just a few key points from this chapter, let them be these

1 When we are born, the external genitalia, chromosomes, hormone levels and our internal reproductive organs that we exhibit are assigned to a sex. However, the sex we are appointed with may not always correlate to our gender.

2 People can be divided into two groups: cisgender and trans. Cisgender aligns with the gender they were assigned with at birth, whilst trans is an umbrella term appointed to those whose gender differs from the gender given to them based on their sex. Within the trans category there are also different umbrellas and identities.

3 Although related, our sexual orientation and our gender are separate. Whilst gender focuses on how we see ourselves, sexual orientation is the basis of who we are physically, emotionally and/or romantically attracted to.

4 We are going to interact with trans kids. Our kids are too. We need to make sure that we proactively educate them and ourselves so we can become part of the solution. We still live in a society that is very resistant to the trans reality.

5 Accepting that there are realities beyond the gender bimodal structure is liberating for the whole of society. Not only does it not weaken the fight of equality, but it is a way to achieve that equality.

What to do next

- Same here as for everyone else except more important! Make sure they have non-binary people in their life (it doesn't have to be physically present, it can be through books, videos, etc.). Talk about it with normality, in a language adapted to what they can understand: 'there are people that are both a boy and a girl, and some people are none of those' and don't make a big deal of it. Just introduce it as part of the reality, because it is.
- If your kids ask you about someone's gender, ask them what they think and why. Explore with them what rules they are applying and try to expand them, try to include the idea that sometimes we don't know the gender until people tell us and that is ok. Ask them what would change for them, why they think it is important to know.
- Don't expect non-binary people to look or act in a certain way to check the boxes in a list. Nobody owes anyone to be female/masculine enough ... there is not one way to be non-binary, the same way that there is not one way to be a woman, or a man. Kids learn while watching us, they will replicate the things that they hear or see at home. So let's lead with kindness.
- There are a lot of books about the topic, for adults and kids. There are lots of free resources online. There are lots of podcasts. The chances of us never having to deal with non-binary people in the context of our children (if not themselves, their friends, or their cousins, or a classmate) are almost nil, we can choose to proactively learn more about it.

Here are some books on the topic.

For kids

- *Julian is a Mermaid* by Jessica Love
- *Little People. Big Dreams: David Bowie* by Maria Isabel Sanchez Vegara
- *Little People. Big Dreams: Ru Paul* by Maria Isabel Sanchez Vegara
- *Red: A Crayon's Story* by Michael Hall
- *Are You a Boy or Are You a Girl?* by Sarah Savage

For adults

- *The Transgender Issue* by Shon Faye
- *Trans Like Me: A Journey for All of Us* by C. N. Lester
- *Life Isn't Binary: On Being Both, Beyond and In-between* by Alex Iantaffi and Meg-John Barker
- *Gender Queer* by Maia Kobabe
- *A Quick and Easy Guide to They/Them Pronouns* by Archie Bongiovanni and Tristan Jimerson
- *Beyond the Gender Binary* by Alok Vaid-Menon

11

Now what?

I always wanted to be a mother. I don't remember considering other options, even when we were having problems conceiving. I always knew I wanted to have two children and I am so lucky to have Eric and Nora – but I am not going to lie, this is much harder than I thought it would be. The pressure of doing everything perfectly is exhausting and, even if we are all in the same boat, parenting still feels lonely sometimes.

I want both my kids to know that being a parent is great, but that it can also be really tough. More importantly, I want them to know that it's just one of many options. I want them to know that they don't have to be parents; they can be whole and complete without having kids. I never presume that they will follow that road, and I don't want them to see it as a given. With hindsight, I wish I had known more about motherhood beforehand; I feel that it was a less informed choice, an option, than I would like it to be for Eric and Nora. I imagine I would have still made the same decision; I don't regret being a mother, but the journey wouldn't have been as shocking.

When I pictured myself as a mother, I always thought I would parent in a very similar way to my parents. I fell into the trap of 'we did it like this and you haven't turned out that bad'. Somehow replicating the things that you have experienced, under the premise that we haven't turned out so bad, feels like we are showing love and respect to our parents. Sometimes defying how we have been brought up feels like a direct confrontation and lack of gratitude. It took me a while to realize that you can be very grateful for how your parents raised you, because they did their best, and still want more for your own kids. You can even wish you had more yourself. When we know better, we do better. I also hope that my children do better than me if they ever have kids. The world is constantly changing and the progress and new learnings and values undoubtedly affect the way we parent. We also tend to overcompensate for things that we missed out on or that we had too much of in our unstoppable search to be perfect. We are given this huge responsibility and sometimes the pressure becomes a burden.

The one thing that I know is that both when we get things right AND when we get things wrong, we are trying our best, and that is enough. There is a huge pressure at the moment on getting everything exactly right with the overdose of information that we have and the pressures of social media and oversharing. But we won't. Let's all make peace with that, we can't do it perfectly, and that's ok. Our parents got a lot of things wrong and here we are, not that bad after all, if we ask them. This book, or any other book about parenting, should not be about doing things right, but about doing things better. And for extra peace of mind I can assure you that in 50 years when we know better and the world we know looks different, we will require a different approach. There will be plenty of time for our kids to blame us for what we did wrong, don't worry!

This is the last chapter and for me it is very important that you don't feel pressured or overwhelmed at this point. Obviously, there is work to do and there are things we can implement in our homes to soften the messages that the world sends out so loudly. I hope that this book encourages you to do things outside your home, too, applying the ideas to other aspects of your life, starting with yourself. But – and this is important – I also know that this is not a job that we will finish in this generation, and that any of our children who become parents themselves will have work to do too. And their kids after them.

This book is an open invitation to be part of the change, hopefully a kind of lightbulb that shines a light on things from a different perspective, and a reliable manual, with tools, that helps navigate that awareness. Please, also take this book as an official reminder that as parents we can't fix the world for our kids, not completely, although trying to do so is thrilling.

During the whole book we've presented activities specifically designed for the content of each chapter. Maybe you have started to implement some of those. Maybe you were waiting to finish the full book before taking action, and I hope you are eager to begin. But where do we start?

The most important message, and the step for everything else, is to acknowledge that in the debate of nature versus nurture, nature is actually taking a lot of undeserved credit. Once we are able to see that certain choices and behaviours in our children are not necessarily who they naturally are, but who they have been taught to be, we will be more prone to broaden those options for them, to educate them in a more free space where they can be themselves.

Seeing the different messaging that bombards them from all angles and understanding that it all adds up makes it very easy to understand the huge effect on kids and their development, and that is where we begin. If we don't see it, then we can't untangle it and try to correct, or at least clarify, it. As I said before, this might come as a bit of a burden because it goes against the blissfulness of ignorance. But it is needed. If you are not there yet, in the beginning you might find that you need to proactively look for things, but don't worry, I am afraid that soon enough you will see all these things without looking for them, which will make the other tasks easier and more natural, even if you also find yourself getting more angry!

Start small. Do one exercise of mindfully searching for gender stereotypes in one thing. Just one.

- Open a children's book and read it with the intention of seeing how many stereotypes you can find both in the drawings and the stories. The way they are dressed, the roles they have, the way they speak, who is the main leader, the different distributions between female and male characters. This is not a moral judgement on the book or the writer, you don't have to burn, ban or even stop liking the book. This is a simple exercise in awareness.

- Watch one episode of a children's show (or five minutes of adverts on a children's channel, if you dare). Do it with the aim of only spotting gender stereotypes. Detective work, 'picking holes' if you would. It is ok if you feel that these stereotypes are not damaging, but just note them anyway. At this stage it is only important to find them, to see them for what they are.

- Do the same, proactively, with a clothes catalogue. Or get yourself into a children's clothes shop and walk around analysing the messages, touching the fabrics, comparing the lengths, the styles, imagining the activities that they will be perfect for, the compliments that kids will receive when wearing them. Do it mindfully, take as little or as much as you want, but just let it sink in.

- Now is the time for toys. Go to a shop and start thinking about which toy is aimed at who. How do you know? What coding is making you feel that way? And what are those toys about? What do they encourage? What skills and messaging do they pass along? Once again, it is not about dividing the toys into good or bad, or fun or boring, or justifying why they are divided that way. It is about getting mindfully immersed in the gender stereotypes and messaging that surrounds our kids.

- Listen to a conversation with children – it can be in the house, it can be with your own kids, it can be in films, or with any children in your family or friendship group. Just listen.

Listen to how they are spoken to, listen to the words that are said, the tone. Check what is celebrated, the adjectives used. Just listen, once again, mindfully.

If you do all those – and of course you can repeat them as many times as you need, or want to – you will see that kids are exposed daily to a multitude of stereotypes and gender messaging. If you start seeing and noticing them, you will also realize how quickly they all add up. How they are not part of a vacuum. Those messages don't exist only in the five minutes during which you are mindfully paying attention, they don't exist only on that one t-shirt in that one shop, nor in that one part of the story in that one book. They exist, at different levels, in so many different things. And unfortunately, there is such a big chain of these subliminal messages coming from everywhere that people and children don't need to be at all mindful to absorb them.

If you focus only on one of the things, let's say one sexist toy that was given by a well-intentioned uncle, it seems a bit dramatic to think that it will affect your child. It probably won't. That one toy is not THE problem, the toy is a cause and a consequence of the real problem. But we cannot fully understand it until we see the parts as pieces of the whole pie. We need to see that toy in the context of being one of many, and sexist toys just as one of many ways to pass information, side-by-side with the other ways, all pushing in the same direction. So, the solution is not to ban or to throw away the toy (I won't judge you if you do, though), the solution is to diversify the other messages and to proactively open conversations that encourage critical thinking. That is the key: critical thinking.

We are not very used to critical thinking, especially because we are quickly led to believe that there are strong natural reasons to justify the differences, and we want to believe it, as it is so much more palatable than questioning everything, including some of our decisions, from a new perspective. It is quite easy to believe that because some women give birth, all women are more caring; it is really tempting to justify aggressive traits in men because thousands of years ago they were the main hunters. But isn't society much more complex than that?

I am not saying that there are not differences, natural differences, between men and women, that is not what this book is about. But it is about analysing how the social differences are much bigger than the natural ones, why it happens, why that is not good for anyone, and what we can do about it. This book is about a way to parent in which we don't focus on the natural differences between boys and girls, rather we celebrate the bigger and more interesting natural differences between each and every one of us. This is a book to encourage parents and carers to embrace critical thinking, so we can pass that critical approach to the next generation.

Asking ourselves 'why', and teaching our children always to look further, is a life skill that not only will help them with the limitations that a society based on binary gender creates, but also with the rest of the expectations and stereotypes that they will inevitably come across in any other area. We want to teach them to explore their identity as something unique and open to possibilities, instead of pre-shaped, and we want them to question the answers of 'because it has always been like that' that they will encounter.

Basically, we need to teach our children to apply their favourite question, WHY?, to their associations of masculine and feminine, and we need to go with them on that journey.

I do workshops in schools. I have been doing them for a while and I have done the same exercise with thousands of kids, both in Northern Ireland and Spain, and always with brilliant results. I separate them into groups of two or three (to facilitate debates and conversations) and I give each group the same list with words on it. 'Butterfly', 'music', 'dog', 'intelligence', 'pink', 'yellow', 'dinosaur' – a variety of things heavily perceived as masculine, feminine or neutral – and they have to fill in their sheet, noting down if it is for girls, for boys or for everyone. I then pick up the papers and we openly discuss the answers. I don't give them an answer, I just ask them to walk me through theirs and invite others to challenge it, and I guide the conversation, mostly with a 'why?'.

For example, I would ask 'what about unicorns?' and most groups would shout 'GIRLS!'. I then give the opportunity to any group that thinks something different to explain why and see how they interact in a mini-debate. If they need an extra adult hand or nobody is choosing to defend the opposite, I find it very useful to afford them the role of them teaching me. 'Ok, I get it … so my son Eric likes horses and that's ok, right? I shouldn't do anything about it, but if the horse has a horn on the forehead then it is no longer ok and I should stop him from liking that horse, because it is not good for boys. That makes sense, thanks, I think he is not going to like it when I tell him, but nothing I can do, right? If it is for girls, it is for girls' and they all panic: 'NOOOOO, don't tell him that', and they see the absurdity of the extreme.

Same with the dinosaurs. 'Ok, raise your hands if you have been to the museum and saw the bones of Dippy the dinosaur. That was cool, right? And now raise your hands if you liked it … wow, I'm very confused – I liked it, and I am a girl, and I thought maybe I was wrong, but it seems that a lot of girls in this class liked it, too … do you think we are all wrong? Because you said that dinosaurs are for boys.'

Kids always come along on the journey, even the ones that are super strict or stubborn at the beginning. Kids always have a moment in which they see it so clearly. If only it were so easy with adults! With the kids we keep talking and debating until we are all in agreement that everything is for everyone, and you can see the excitement in their faces, it does feel like you unlocked something. They now all get it, they are all part of this new discovery that they have made themselves.

Another exercise I do with them, after we are all happy to let the stereotypes go, is asking them about a time in which they were told, or they felt that they couldn't do or like something, just because of their gender, and how they felt about it. A lot of boys open up about wanting to play with their sisters' dolls and being ridiculed, or wearing certain things; girls talk about not being allowed to play football because the boys won't let them, and so on. Things that you would expect to be 'so last year' are still here. I have done this workshop in both lower and higher socioeconomic status groups, in Spain and in Belfast, and there are more similarities than differences regarding kids still feeling held back. We always end the sessions with a promise that not only will we remember that everything is for everyone but that we will be the superheroes making sure everyone else knows it, too!

I love those sessions; I love the high I get from them and the hopes they give me for the future. The feedback from parents and teachers is really positive, and there are always a couple of kids at the end of it who come to tell me something they didn't feel that they could openly share in front of their class but they want to get off their chest. They crave reassurance, for someone to tell them 'you have every right to be yourself, there is nothing wrong with it'.

As much as I love and believe in the impact of that work, I also know that it is not enough – that the effects and the excitement of a life full of choices and without a right or wrong path will start fading as soon as one of their parents tells them that it is nonsense, or as soon as the peer pressure outside the session kicks in. These kind of messages need to be reinforced daily if we want them to have a chance of winning through in the struggle against the omnipresent stereotypes.

The other important thing is understanding that our other main job is acting as positive role models. Even if children rebel (as they will) and out-grow us (as they will) we still need to remember that they will develop under the pillars that we set.

Their idea of what a family is, what love and respect is, our roles as people, how we speak to each other and so on will all be shaped by what they see from the adults in their life.

If at home we have very strictly gender-stereotyped ways of operating, even if we tell our kids that they can and have to break through these stereotypes, what they understand and see as normal will always carry more weight. I am not saying 'change the way you live' but do check what kind of messages you are unconsciously passing on and which they will likely repeat by imitation. And maybe see how it would feel for you to ask 'why?' and to see if there is another way.

Are the house chores more or less evenly split? Do you divide tasks in a stereotyped way? Are the kids' chores going to be the same regardless of their gender? Are all the careers choices respected in the same way? If you watch sport, do you watch only men's sport? When you are around friends and family are you all normally split by gender? Do your kids see a variety of adult friendships? Is appearance and physical beauty in women something that is talked about in front of them often? Are sexist jokes normalized because 'it's just a joke'? What would an alien who has never been on earth before understand about what being a woman and what being a man is from staying in your house for a couple of days?

When avoiding the problems is just not possible, critical thinking and role modelling are the two biggest things we can do to reduce the impact.

If you have read this far in the book, you already know. In fairness, if you started reading this book at all you already cared, and that's a lot. I am convinced we are going in the right direction, I am positive that all the small things that don't seem to matter are making a huge impact on the next generations, and I am sure that our kids will become great, caring, kind leaders who will do better.

We are all part of the same solution, and that's exciting. I know we are also part of the same problem, but let's focus on the positive. We are all part of the same solutions – for years and centuries, men and women have been determined to change things. Some have rioted, others have set boundaries at home, some have lobbied, others have carried out experiments, some have parented in a way that they would have liked to have been parented. We are all part of the same solution, and our kids are our best and biggest chance of fuelling the change.

I want to change the world for my kids, of course, but it is great to know that my biggest impact will be to bring up responsible and open-minded kids. It is great to know that changing the world is not only something we will do for them but is something we will do together with them, and something they will carry forward after we are gone.

Expert interview: Catherine Bailey

Catherine Bailey is the founder of Think or Blue, a community of parents, teachers and family who strive to raise and educate children free from gender stereotypes. She helps caregivers use feminist parenting strategies to tackle tough topics like body image, consent and media literacy, to raise kind, compassionate children who embrace their individuality, and are ready to change the world.

Catherine is a lawyer and gender equity expert and was instrumental in passing policies that support work and family, such as pay equity and paid family and medical leave, in her home state of Connecticut.

Raised in the 1980s on *Free to Be You and Me*, Catherine has feminism running in her blood. She lives in Connecticut (halfway in between Boston and New York) with her husband and 5-year-old, and loves dark chocolate, rock concerts and Gilmore Girls.

Find free resources and guides at <www.thinkorblue.com>.

Why did you start working on the impact of gender stereotypes in kids and why was it important for you?

When I was pregnant, I pounded on my keyboard to write 'Why I Didn't Find Out the Sex of My Baby', a piece intended to shake out my personal frustrations. The article sat there, untouched, for a couple more years, until I founded Think or Blue in 2017. But in that moment of pregnancy, the importance of my unborn baby's genitals to complete strangers felt bizarre. My husband and I chose not to find out the sex of our future baby, and people's reactions were mixed. Several people pressed us for details and asked how we would manage to prepare, as if our major decisions hinged on the baby's anatomy.

The truth is, we didn't make this choice as expectant parents because we simply love surprises. Not at all. We made this choice knowing that society was desperate to impose ideas and expectations upon our unborn child based on ingrained biases and outdated stereotypes about children's personalities, interests and future potential.

As I've said before, you can draw a wavy line from gender reveal parties to the wage gap. The pink and blue toys and clothes don't simply disappear after childhood. The effects remain. We see the effects in job segregation, sexual violence, pay inequity, discrimination in the workplace, and the imbalanced division of labour in households. And it doesn't just impact women. We tell young boys not to feel their feelings and instruct them to deny anything less than 'masculine', then we're surprised when men disproportionately engage in violence. We shouldn't be.

As a life-long feminist and 'take-action' sort of person, I knew I had to do something about the pervasive gender stereotypes that impact our children before they've taken their first breath outside the womb. Think or Blue was an important next step for me to both awaken people's unconscious stereotypes and connect with feminist parents throughout the world who care deeply about raising children who embrace who they are and are ready to change the world.

During your research and journey as an expert, what was the biggest WOW moment you had, or what was the piece of research that had the biggest impact on you?

Interestingly, the piece of research that impacted me most was not focused solely on children. With my background in law, women's issues and policy, I was co-chairing the Connecticut Campaign for Paid Family Leave in 2013 during my tenure as Deputy Director of the Connecticut Women's Education and Legal Fund and learned that one in four new birth mothers returns to work just two weeks after birth in the US. Two weeks! I was naively shocked by this statistic. Even though we were eventually successful in passing a universal paid family and medical leave law in Connecticut in 2019, the US remains far behind the rest of the world in terms of caregiving.

For me, this statistic about new parents reflected so many stereotypes, oppressions and injustices all rolled into one. It showed our society's collective failure to value caregiving, or any work or activities that we deem 'feminine'. It demonstrated our inability to recognize men as parents and caregivers and support their need and desire to care for their families. It revealed racial disparities in health care that result in a childbirth mortality rate for Black women at four times the rate of white women. These issues are simply unacceptable and need our attention.

Policy work is critical for communities to work toward equitable rights. But just as important, maybe even more so, is a shift in opinion. Will we ever reach true equity without a massive change in public opinion? To me, the answer is no. And so it made sense to start with the next generation and their caregivers.

Interestingly, though, our personal experiences may be just as motivating as research, and sometimes just as shocking. Perhaps my biggest WOW moment in this feminist parenting journey was when a stranger spoke to my child, 18 months old at the time, at a park. He spoke to her with the utmost confidence and assurance. It was staggering – his tone of voice was markedly different from the way most adults spoke to my child. I realized, based on my toddler's clothes and hat (which happened to be shades of blue that day), that the adult mistook her for a boy.

Until that point, most adults used delicate, gentle voices with her, exclaiming about her cuteness. It was then that I realized how differently people speak to men and boys. The internal biases were crystal clear.

While I harboured no ill feelings toward this individual whatsoever, this teeny, seemingly insignificant moment at the park fuelled my desire to change the way we treat and perceive people based on their outward appearance.

In terms of parents as principal educators, if you were to give them two or three practical things that they could start doing right now at home, what would those be?

The three easiest ways that parents can engage in feminist parenting are:

1 **Examine your biases.** Even lifelong feminists, womanists and scholars of oppression must continually unearth their own biases. When your child falls down, gets hurt or makes mischief, what is your reaction? Would it be any different if your child identified as a different gender? I ask myself this question constantly. Bias doesn't mean we're bad people, it simply means society has conditioned us.

2 **Look at your household roles.** This tip is most critical for male–female household partnerships. Who does the majority of the childcare and the housework? Are your chores segregated by traditional stereotypes? Who does most of the mental and emotional labour (e.g. planning the social schedule and comforting children when they're sad)?

3 **Enrich representation.** Look not only at your child's books and toys but to their community. Who do they see represented? Who is most frequently the protagonist or the hero? Do their surroundings include people of all races, genders, abilities,

sexual orientations and body shapes? Books are the easiest place to start – commit to only borrowing books from the library that feature identities that are lacking in your home.

For those parents wishing to learn more, are there any particular websites (apart from yours!), books, videos, podcasts or other resources you would recommend to help them?

There are a lot – it's difficult not getting carried away. Here are just some of my favourites:

- Gender Equality Collective
- Future Feminists
- Read Like a Rock Star
- Not Only Pink and Blue
- Britt Hawthorne
- Dr Gina Rippon
- Let Toys Be Toys
- ManEnough.com and their series of videos
- Documentary: *The Mask You Live In*
- Little Justice Leaders

If you take away just a few key points from this chapter, let them be these

1 Parenting isn't easy and everything won't always be done right, but it's important that the journey of parenting is ever-growing and continuously aspiring to do better.
2 Critical thinking not only paves the way for breaking down gender stereotypes but it will help kids to question the things that we take for granted and have a richer range of choices.
3 Allowing space for kids to be themselves without the constrictions of stereotypes empowers them and unlocks their potential, which is great for them and for society as a whole.
4 Parents are role models for their children and have a powerful impact upon them as they continue to grow. Their change starts with our change.

What to do next

There are plenty of activities throughout the book and this chapter itself for you to choose from so, to close things off, after the references is some free space for you to make notes and add other ideas that you might see around from other books, social media, or just your own reflections.

I encourage you, as suggested in Chapter 2, to also use this space to make notes of stereotypes that you start spotting that maybe you didn't before, to start 'collecting' them to have your own personal records of things that you perceive differently based on gender. If you are passing this book around to carers, teachers or family, you might also use this space to add some specific comments that you want to be taken into account for your specific child. Things that for you are very important, or things that apply directly to them or you have noticed in them.

Whatever you use this space for I hope it feels like an encouragement to act. I hope by now you have not only the information and the emotions but also the excitement to start putting things into place, to start making changes and observing things with different lenses.

I would personally love to hear more from you and bring this conversation forward, so share your thoughts, ideas and questions to social media and make sure you tag @virginia-mendezm or hashtag #childhoodunlimited.

References

1 Ainsworth, C. (2015). Sex redefined. *Nature, 518*, 288–291. https://doi.org/10.1038/518288a

2 Hida. (2015, April 1). *How Common Is Intersex? An Explanation of the Stats*. IC4E. https://www.intersexequality. com/how-common-is-intersex-in-humans/

3 Hildreth, C. (2021, August 14). *The Gender Spectrum: A Scientist Explains Why Gender Isn't Binary*. https:// cadehildreth.com/gender-spectrum/

4 Rippon, G. (2016). The trouble with girls? *The Psychologist*. https://thepsychologist.bps.org.uk/volume-29/ december-2016/trouble-girls. Citing May, A. (2011). Experience-dependent structural plasticity in the adult human brain. *Trends in Cognitive Sciences, 15*(10), 475–482. Shors, T. J. (2016). A trip down memory lane about sex differences in the brain. *Philosophical Transactions of the Royal Society B*. doi: 10.1098/rstb.2015.0124

5 Hölzel, B. K., Carmody, J., Vangel, M., Congleton, C., Yerramsetti, S. M., Gard, T., & Lazar, S. W. (2011). Mindfulness practice leads to increases in regional brain gray matter density. *Psychiatry Research: Neuroimaging, 191*(1), 36–43. https://doi.org/10.1016/j.pscychresns.2010.08.006

6 Wraga, M., Helt, M., Jacobs, E., & Sullivan, K. (2007). Neural basis of stereotype-induced shifts in women's mental rotation performance. *Social Cognitive and Affective Neuroscience, 2*(1), 12–19.

7 Hackman, D. A., & Farah, M. J. (2009). Socioeconomic status and the developing brain. *Trends in Cognitive Sciences, 13*(2), 65–73. https://doi.org/10.1016/j.tics.2008.11.003

8 Gianaros, P. J., Horenstein, J. A., Cohen, S., Matthews, K. A., Brown, S. M., Flory, J. D., Critchley, H. D., Manuck, S. B., & Hariri, A. R. (2007). Perigenual anterior cingulate morphology covaries with perceived social standing. *Social*

Cognitive and Affective Neuroscience, 2(3), 161–173. https://doi.org/10.1093/scan/nsm013

9 Rippon, G., Jordan-Young, R., Kaiser, A., & Fine, C. (2014). Recommendations for sex/gender neuroimaging research: Key principles and implications for research design, analysis, and interpretation. *Frontiers in Human Neuroscience, 8.* https://doi.org/10.3389/fnhum.2014.00650

10 Joel, D., Berman, Z., Tavor, I., Wexler, N., Gaber, O., Stein, Y., Shefi, N., Pool, J., Urchs, S., Margulies, D. S., Liem, F., Hänggi, J., Jäncke, L., & Assaf, Y. (2015). Sex beyond the genitalia: The human brain mosaic. *Proceedings of the National Academy of Sciences, 112*(50), 15468–15473. https://doi.org/10.1073/pnas.1509654112

11 Joel, D., & Fausto-Sterling, A. (2016). Beyond sex differences: New approaches for thinking about variation in brain structure and function. *Philosophical Transactions of the Royal Society B: Biological Sciences, 371*(1688), 20150451. https://doi.org/10.1098/rstb.2015.0451

12 Reis, H. T., & Carothers, B. J. (2014). Black and white or shades of gray: Are gender differences categorical or dimensional? *Current Directions in Psychological Science, 23*(1), 19–26. https://doi.org/10.1177/0963721413504105

13 Hebb, D. O. (1949). *The Organization of Behavior.* Wiley & Sons, New York.

14 Rippon, G. (2019, February 28). *The Gendered Brain: Pink and Blue or Fifty Shades of Grey Matter?* Aston University. https://www2.aston.ac.uk/news/?the-gendered-brain-pink-and-blue-or-fifty-shades-of-grey-matte

15 Fine, C., Jordan-Young, R., Kaiser, A., & Rippon, G. (2013). Plasticity, plasticity, plasticity... and the rigid problem of sex. *Trends in Cognitive Sciences, 17*(11), 550–551.

16 Ellemers, N. (2018). Gender stereotypes. *Annual Review of Psychology, 69*(1), 275–298. https://doi.org/10.1146/annurev-psych-122216-011719

17 Stephens-Davidowitz, S. (2014, January 19). Opinion | Google, tell me. Is my son a genius? *The New York Times.* https://www.nytimes.com/2014/01/19/opinion/sunday/ google-tell-me-is-my-son-a-genius.html

18 Department for Education (2019, February). *Attitudes towards STEM subjects by gender at KS4.* UK Government Dept for Education. https://assets.publishing.service.gov. uk/government/uploads/system/uploads/attachment_data/ file/913311/Attitudes_towards_STEM_subjects_by_gender_ at_KS4.pdf

19 Bloodhart, B., Balgopal, M. M., Casper, A. M. A., Sample McMeeking, L. B., & Fischer, E. V. (2020). Outperforming yet undervalued: Undergraduate women in STEM. *PLoS ONE, 15*(6), e0234685. https://doi.org/10.1371/journal. pone.0234685

20 Swim, J. K., & Sanna, L. J. (1996). He's skilled, she's lucky: A meta-analysis of observers' attributions for women's and men's successes and failures. *Personality and Social Psychology Bulletin, 22*(5), 507–519. https://doi. org/10.1177/0146167296225008

21 Cherry, K. (2020, May 15). *The Importance of Assimilation in Adaptation.* Very Well Mind. https://www.verywellmind. com/what-is-assimilation-2794821

22 Chatard, A., Guimond, S., & Selimbegovic, L. (2007). 'How good are you in math?' The effect of gender stereotypes on students' recollection of their school marks. *Journal of Experimental Social Psychology, 43*-(6),1017–1024. https:// linkinghub.elsevier.com/retrieve/pii/S0022103106001673

23 Tiedemann, J. (2000). Gender-related beliefs of teachers in elementary school mathematics. *Educational Studies in Mathematics 41*, 191–207. https://doi. org/10.1023/A:1003953801526

24 Kersey, A. J., Braham, E. J., Csumitta, K. D., Libertus, M. E., & Cantlon, J. F. (2018). No intrinsic gender differences in children's earliest numerical abilities. *Npj Science*

of Learning, 3(1). https://doi.org/10.1038/s41539-018-0028-7 and Hutchison, J. E., Lyons, I. M. & Ansari, D. (2018). More similar than different: Gender differences in children's basic numerical skills are the exception not the rule. *Child Development, 90*(1). https://doi.org/10.1111/cdev.13044

25 Lindberg, S. M., Hyde, J. S., Petersen, J. L., & Linn, M. C. (2010). New trends in gender and mathematics performance: A meta-analysis. *Psychological Bulletin, 136*(6), 1123–1135. https://doi.org/10.1037/a0021276

26 Ibid.

27 van Mier, H. I., Schleepen, T. M. J., & van den Berg, F. C. G. (2019). Gender differences regarding the impact of math anxiety on arithmetic performance in second and fourth graders. *Frontiers in Psychology, 9*. https://doi.org/10.3389/fpsyg.2018.02690

28 Stephens, N. M., & Levine, C. S. (2011). Opting out or denying discrimination? How the framework of free choice in American society influences perceptions of gender inequality. *Psychological Science, 22*(10), 1231–1236. https://doi.org/10.1177/0956797611417260

29 Handley, I. M., Brown, E. R., Moss-Racusin, C. A., & Smith, J. L. (2015). Quality of evidence revealing subtle gender biases in science is in the eye of the beholder. *Proceedings of the National Academy of Sciences, 112*(43), 13201–13206. https://doi.org/10.1073/pnas.1510649112

30 McCabe, J., Fairchild, E., Grauerholz, L., Pescosolido, B. A., & Tope, D. (2011). Gender in twentieth-century children's books. *Gender & Society, 25*(2), 197–226. https://doi.org/10.1177/0891243211398358

31 DeLoache, J. S., Cassidy, D.J., & Carpenter, C. J. (1987). The three bears are all boys: Mothers' gender labeling of neutral picture book characters. *Sex Roles 17*, 163–178. https://doi.org/10.1007/BF00287623

32 Arthur, A. G., & White, H. (1996). Children's assignment of gender to animal characters in pictures. *The Journal of Genetic Psychology, 157*(3), 297–301. https://doi.org/10.1080/00221325.1996.9914867

33 McCabe, J., Fairchild, E., Grauerholz, L., Pescosolido, B. A., & Tope, D. (2011). Gender in twentieth-century children's books: Patterns of disparity in titles and central characters. *Gender & Society, 25*(2), 197–226. https://doi.org/10.1177/0891243211398358

34 Caldwell, E., & Wilbraham, S. (2019, August 14). *Meeting Gender in Space: Visual Imagery in Children's Science Books.* In: EASST, Lancaster University. https://eprints.lancs.ac.uk/id/eprint/135539/

35 Fitzpatrick, M. J., & McPherson, B. J. (2010). Coloring within the lines: Gender stereotypes in contemporary coloring books. *Sex Roles, 62*, 127–137. https://doi.org/10.1007/s11199-009-9703-8

36 Jackson, S., & Gee, S. (2005). 'Look Janet', 'No you look John': Constructions of gender in early school reader illustrations across 50 years. *Gender and Education, 17*(2), 115–128. https://doi.org/10.1080/0954025042000301410

37 (Spitz 1999, cited in Frawley 2008: 291). Frawley, T. J. (2008), Gender schema and prejudicial recall: How children misremember, fabricate, and distort gendered picture book information, *Journal of Research in Childhood Education, 22*(3), 291–303. doi:10.1080/02568540809594628

38 *Watching Gender: How Stereotypes in Movies and on TV Impact Kids' Development.* Common Sense Media. https://www.commonsensemedia.org/research/watching-gender

39 Baker, K., & Raney, A. A. (2007). Equally super?: Gender-role stereotyping of superheroes in children's animated programs. *Mass Communication and Society, 10*(1), 25–41. https://doi.org/10.1080/15205430709337003 and Stern, D. M. (2005). MTV, reality television and the commodification of female sexuality in The Real World. *Media Report to Women, 33*, 13–21.

40   Dohnt, H., & Tiggemann, M. (2006). The contribution of peer and media influences to the development of body satisfaction and self-esteem in young girls: A prospective study. *Developmental Psychology, 42*(5), 929–936. https://psycnet.apa.org/buy/2006-11399-014

41   Fredrickson, B. L., & Roberts, T. A. (1997). Objectification theory: Toward understanding women's lived experiences and mental health risks. *Psychology of Women Quarterly, 21*(2), 173–206. https://doi.org/10.1111/j.1471-6402.1997.tb00108.x

42   Pacilli, M. G., Tomasetto, C., & Cadinu, M. (2016). Exposure to sexualized advertisements disrupts children's math performance by reducing working memory. *Sex Roles, 74*, 389–398. https://doi.org/10.1007/s11199-016-0581-6

43   Grabe, S., & Hyde, J. S. (2009). Body objectification, MTV, and psychological outcomes among female adolescents. *Journal of Applied Social Psychology, 39*(12), 2840–2858. https://doi.org/10.1111/j.1559-1816.2009.00552.x

44   Tiggemann, M., & Slater, A. (2015). The role of self-objectification in the mental health of early adolescent girls: Predictors and Consequences, *Journal of Pediatric Psychology, 40*(7), 704–711. https://doi.org/10.1093/jpepsy/jsv021

45   Wroblewski, R., & Huston, A. C. (1987). Televised occupational stereotypes and their effects on early adolescents: Are they changing? *The Journal of Early Adolescence, 7*(3), 283–297. https://doi.org/10.1177/0272431687073005

46   Bond, B. J. (2016). Fairy godmothers > robots: The Influence of Televised Gender Stereotypes and Counter-Stereotypes on Girls' Perceptions of STEM. *Bulletin of Science, Technology & Society, 36*(2), 91–97. https://doi.org/10.1177/0270467616655951

47   Heldman, C. et al. (2020). *Historic Screen Time and Speaking Time for Female Characters.* See Jane 2020 TV Report. The

Geena Davis Institute for Gender in Media. https://seejane.org/research-informs-empowers/2020-tv-historic-screen-time-speaking-time-for-female-characters/

48   Heldman, C. *et al.* (2020). *Historic Gender Parity in Family Films*. See Jane **2020** Report. The Geena Davis Institute for Gender in Media at Mount St. Mary's. https://seejane.org/research-informs-empowers/2020-film-historic-gender-parity-in-family-films/

49   *If He Can See It, Will He Be It?* (2018). The Geena Davis Institute for Gender in Media https://seejane.org/research-informs-empowers/if-he-can-see-it-will-he-be-it/

50   *Is TV Making Your Child Prejudiced? A Report into Pre-school Programming.* Hopster. https://hopster_wordpress_v2.storage.googleapis.com/Hopster-Predjudice-Report-DIGITAL.pdf

51   Lemish, D. (2010). *Screening Gender on Children's Television: The Views of Producers around the World (1st ed.).* Routledge, London. https://doi.org/10.4324/9780203855409

52   *Research Informs & Empowers.* The Geena Davis Institute for Gender in Media https://seejane.org/research-informs-empowers/

53   Washington, L. (2019, December 29). *The Importance of Representation in Film and Media.* Medium.com. https://medium.com/@Laurenwash/the-importance-of-representation-in-film-and-media-2d006149cac9

54   Smith, A. (Host) (2020–present). *Girls on Film* [Audio Podcast]. Apple podcasts. https://podcasts.apple.com/gb/podcast/girls-on-film/id1439182513?mt=2

55   *Toys and Learning in the EYFS. Let Toys Be Toys.* https://lettoysbetoys.org.uk/resources/toys-and-learning/

56   *What the Research Says: Gender-Typed Toys.* NAEYC. https://www.naeyc.org/resources/topics/play/gender-typed-toys

57   Bradbard, M. R., Martin, C. L., Endsley, R. C., & Halverson, C. F. (1986). Influence of sex stereotypes on children's exploration and memory: A competence versus

performance distinction. *Developmental Psychology, 22*(4), 481–486. https://psycnet.apa.org/record/1986-29670-001

58 Shell, R., & Eisenberg, N. (1990). The role of peers' gender in children's naturally occurring interest in toys. *International Journal of Behavioral Development, 13*(3), 373–388. https://journals.sagepub.com/doi/10.1177/016502549001300309

59 Montemayor, R. (1974). Children's performance in a game and their attraction to it as a function of sex-typed labels. *Child Development, 45,* 152–156. https://www.semanticscholar.org/paper/Children%27s-Performance-in-a-Game-and-Their-to-It-as-Montemayor/99ab2e6a4ed63cc9051af6847a36851162a03b80

60 Fiore, J. (2018, December 19). *Why Jesus and Mary Always Wear Red and Blue in Art History.* Artsy. https://www.artsy.net/article/artsy-editorial-jesus-mary-wear-red-blue-art-history

61 Stamberg, S. (2014, April 1). *Girls Are Taught to 'Think Pink,' But That Wasn't Always So.* NPR. https://www.npr.org/2014/04/01/297159948/girls-are-taught-to-think-pink-but-that-wasnt-always-so?t=1623932714369

62 LoBue, V., & DeLoache, J. (2011). Pretty in pink: The early development of gender-stereotyped colour preferences. *The British Journal of Developmental Psychology. 29.* 656–67. https://www.researchgate.net/publication/51578057_Pretty_in_pink_The_early_development_of_gender-stereotyped_colour_preferences

63 Roomes, E. (2020, January 20). *Gender Stereotypes: Slogans on Children's Clothing.* Pink and blue review. https://pinkandbluereview.com/slogans-on-childrens-clothing/

64 Haglund, J. D. (2017, November 16). *Did You Ever Notice This About The Clothes You Grew Up Wearing?* Refinery29. https://www.refinery29.com/en-us/kids-clothing-sexist-message-gender-roles

65 Sarkar, P. (2013, January 1). *Children's Size Chart for Various Clothes by Age and Body Measurement.* Online clothing study. https://www.onlineclothingstudy.com/2013/01/childrens-size-chart-for-variuos.html

66 Clemence, S. (2019, July 30). The gender divide in preschoolers' closets. *The New York Times.* https://www.nytimes.com/2018/08/28/well/family/the-gender-divide-in-preschoolers-closets.html

67 Blazeski, G. (2018, March 20). *Most Victorian-era Boys Wore Dresses and the Reasons Were Practical.* The Vintage News. https://www.thevintagenews.com/2018/03/20/breeching-boys/

68 Editors of Encyclopaedia Britannica. *When Did Women Start Wearing Pants?* Encyclopedia Britannica. https://www.britannica.com/story/when-did-women-start-wearing-pants

69 Agustoni, P. (2018, January 12). *Gender Stereotypes in Children's Clothing.* Raffia. https://raffia-magazine.com/2018/01/12/gender-stereotypes-in-childrens-clothing/

70 *Should We Ban Casual Heels & Wedges for Girls? Yes. Here's Why.* Let Clothes Be Clothes. https://www.letclothesbeclothes.co.uk/post/ban-casual-heels-and-wedges-for-girls-yes-here-s-why

71 Hunt, S. (2017, January 24). The way we talk to girls is different to the way we talk to boys. *The Sydney Morning Herald.* https://www.smh.com.au/lifestyle/the-way-we-talk-to-girls-is-different-from-the-way-we-talk-to-boys-20170123-gtwwm4.html

72 Reby, D., Levréro, F., Gustafsson, E. *et al.* (2016). Sex stereotypes influence adults' perception of babies' cries. *BMC Psychol 4*, 19. https://bmcpsychology.biomedcentral.com/articles/10.1186/s40359-016-0123-6

73 *Women's Pain Is Routinely Underestimated, and Gender Stereotypes Are to Blame – New Research.* The Conversation. https://theconversation.com/womens-pain-is-routinely-underestimated-and-gender-stereotypes-are-to-blame-new-research-158599

74 Aspan, M. (2020, June 30). *'We Can't Ever Go to The Doctor With Our Guard Down': Why Black Women Are 40% More Likely to Die of Breast Cancer.* Fortune. https://fortune.com/2020/06/30/black-women-breast-cancer-mortality-racism-healthcare-pandemic/

75 Leaper, C., Anderson, K. J., & Sanders, P. (1998). Moderators of gender effects on parents' talk to their children: a meta-analysis. *Dev Psychol. 34*(1), 3–27. https://pubmed.ncbi.nlm.nih.gov/9471001/

76 Johnson, K., Caskey, M., Rand, K., Tucker, R., & Vohr, B. (2014). Gender differences in adult-infant communication in the first months of life. *Pediatrics, 134*(6), e1603–e1610. https://pediatrics.aappublications.org/content/134/6/e1603

77 Aznar, A., & Tenenbaum, H. R. (2013). Spanish parents' emotion talk and their children's understanding of emotion. *Frontiers in Psychology, 4.* https://www.frontiersin.org/articles/10.3389/fpsyg.2013.00670/full

78 Leaper, C., Anderson, K. J., & Sanders, P. (1998). Moderators of gender effects on parents' talk to their children: a meta-analysis. *Dev Psychol. 34*(1), 3–27. https://pubmed.ncbi.nlm.nih.gov/9471001/

79 Mascaro, J. S., Rentscher, K. E., Hackett, P. D., Mehl, M. R., & Rilling, J. K. (2017). Child gender influences paternal behavior, language, and brain function. *Behavioral Neuroscience, 131*(3), 262–273. https://www.apa.org/pubs/journals/releases/bne-bne0000199.pdf

80 O'Neal, E. E., Plumert, J. M., & Peterson, C. (2016). Parent–child injury prevention conversations following a trip to the emergency department, *Journal of Pediatric Psychology, 41*(2), 256–264. https://academic.oup.com/jpepsy/article/41/2/256/2579803

81 Shaywitz, B., Shaywitz, S., Pugh, K. *et al.* (1995). Sex differences in the functional organization of the brain for language. *Nature, 373*, 607–609. https://doi.org/10.1038/373607a0

82 Huttenlocher, J., Haight, W., Bryk, A., Seltzer, M., *et al.* (1991). Early vocabulary growth: Relation to language input and gender. *Developmental Psychology, 27*(2), 236–248. https://doi.org/10.1037/0012-1649.27.2.236

83 Barbu, S., Nardy, A., Chevrot, J. P., Guellaï, B., Glas, L., Juhel, J., & Lemasson, A. (2015). Sex differences in language across early childhood: Family socioeconomic status does not impact boys and girls equally. *Front. Psychol., 6,* 1874. https://doi.org/10.3389/fpsyg.2015.01874. Bornstein, M. H., Hahn, C. S., & Haynes, O. M. (2004). Specific and general language performance across early childhood: Stability and gender considerations. *First Language, 24*(3), 267–304. https://doi.org/10.1177/0142723704045681. Lovas, G. S. (2010). Gender and patterns of language development in mother-toddler and father-toddler dyads. *First Language, 31*(1), 83–108. https://doi.org/10.1177/0142723709359241. Wallentin, M. (2020). Gender differences in language are small but matter for disorders. *Handbook of Clinical Neurology, 175*, 81–102. https://doi.org/10.1016/B978-0-444-64123-6.00007-2

84 Marjanovič-Umek, L., & Fekonja-Peklaj, U. (2017). Gender differences in children's language: A meta-analysis of Slovenian studies. *CEPSJ, 7*(2). https://files.eric.ed.gov/fulltext/EJ1145869.pdf

85 Lewis, M., & Lupyan, G. (2020). Gender stereotypes are reflected in the distributional structure of 25 languages. *Nature Human Behaviour, 4*(10), 1021–1028. https://www.nature.com/articles/s41562-020-0918-6.epdf

86 American Psychological Association, Task Force on Issues of Sexual Bias in Graduate Education (1975). Guidelines for nonsexist use of language. *American Psychologist, 30*(6), 682–684. https://doi.org/10.1037/h0076869

87 Hamilton, M. C. (1988). Using masculine generics: Does generic *he* increase male bias in the user's imagery?

Sex Roles, 19, 785–799. https://link.springer.com/
article/10.1007/BF00288993

88 Johnson, K., Caskey, M., Rand, K., Tucker, R., &
Vohr, B. (2014b). Gender differences in adult-infant
communication in the first months of life. *Pediatrics,
134*(6), e1603–e1610. https://pediatrics.aappublications.
org/content/134/6/e1603

89 *Cornell University and Hollaback! Research Survey on Street
Harassment* (2014). Cornell University. https://www.
ihollaback.org/cornell-international-survey-on-street-
harassment/#cr

90 Watts, A. W. (2014, June 2). *Why Does John Get the
STEM Job Rather Than Jennifer?* Stanford University –
The Clayman Institute for Gender Research. https://
gender.stanford.edu/news-publications/gender-news/
why-does-john-get-stem-job-rather-jennifer

91 Hess, C., Ahmed, T., & Hayes, J. (2020). Providing
unpaid household and care work in the United States:
Uncovering inequality. *Institute for Women's Policy
Research.* https://iwpr.org/wp-content/uploads/2020/01/
IWPR-Providing-Unpaid-Household-and-Care-Work-in-the-
United-States-Uncovering-Inequality.pdf

92 Rao, A. H. (2019, May 12). Women breadwinners still
do most of the family's chores. *The Atlantic.* https://
www.theatlantic.com/family/archive/2019/05/
breadwinning-wives-gender-inequality/589237/

93 *UK VC & Female Founders Report* (2020). British Business
Bank. https://www.british-business-bank.co.uk/
uk-vc-female-founders-report/

94 *Suicide.* Ben.org.uk. https://ben.org.uk/our-services/
health-and-wellbeing/top-searches/mens-health/suicide/

95 Rankin, J. (2017, November 29). Fewer women leading
FTSE firms than men called John. The Guardian. https://
www.theguardian.com/business/2015/mar/06/johns-davids-
and-ians-outnumber-female-chief-executives-in-ftse-100

96 McManus, I. (2009). The history and geography of human handedness. In I. Sommer & R. Kahn (Eds.), *Language Lateralization and Psychosis* (pp. 37–58). Cambridge: Cambridge University Press. https://www.cambridge.org/core/books/language-lateralization-and-psychosis/history-and-geography-of-human-handedness/C50A2D64C7147EEE340222E6D2A3776E

97 Ennis, D. (2020, July 15). *Largest Survey of Transgender and Nonbinary Youth Says More Than Half Seriously Considered Suicide.* Forbes. https://www.forbes.com/sites/dawnstaceyennis/2020/07/15/largest-survey-of-transgender-and-nonbinary-youth-says-more-than-half-seriously-considered-suicide/?sh=47f87fe83404

98 *Groups and Resources.* Genderspectrum.org. https://genderspectrum.org/resources

99 Wamsley, L. (2021, June 2). *A Guide to Gender Identity Terms.* NPR. https://www.npr.org/2021/06/02/996319297/gender-identity-pronouns-expression-guide-lgbtq

Index

agender people, 157–8
animal characters in books
  gender bias, 32–4
  pronouns for, 106
animals
  designs on clothing, 84–5
  gender stereotypes, 170
appearance-focused content, 49
assimilation theory, 18
Aston Brain Centre, 8

Bailey, Catherine, 173–7
Barbie, 64
Bates, Laura, 135
BBC
  CBeebies, 45–6
  'No more boys and girls'
    documentary, 7, 106
Beaven, Kirstie, 103–6
Bechdel-Wallace Test, 51–2, 60
Beyond Male Role Models
  (Open University report), 142
Bigler, Rebecca, 24, 25
body image, 49
body shape and clothing, 86–8
books
  about non-binary children,
    163
  addressing gender stereotypes,
    27, 39–42
  choosing, 43–4
  for confidence in girls, 123
  gender bias, 32–8
  gender stereotypes in, 11

illustrations in, 37–8
pronouns for characters, 106
racial diversity, 38
studies of, 32–3, 35–6
writing, 30–2
brain
  affected by gender
    stereotypes, 9–11
  neuroplasticity, 2–5, 8–9
breastfeeding, sexualized
  comments, 131–2
British Film Institute (BFI), 56,
  58

careers
  gender stereotypes in
    language, 102, 105
  represented in books, 36–7
  represented on TV shows,
    49–51, 55
  success in, 116–17
caregivers, gender bias in
  books, 36–7
CBeebies, 45–6
cisgender people, 156
clothing, 78–9
  children's own choices, 80–2
  colours, 82–3, 92–3
  gender stereotypes, 11, 82–91
  gender-neutral, 91–3
  materials, 88–9
  practicalities, 87
  shape, 86–8
  shoes, 89–90

slogans and designs, 83–5
twentieth century, 82–3, 92–3
colour preferences, 6
of clothing, 82–3, 92–3
coding of toys, 67–8
Common Sense Media, 48–50
confidence, 122–3
Confidence Code for Girls, The, 123
consent, 128–9
crushes, 150
crying, 97
Cuddy, Amy, 120
curiosity, 152

Day of the Girl, 120
designs, on clothing, 84–5
Dinella, Professor Lisa, 69
#DiverseEd, 118
Dove Self-Esteem project, 123
dresses, 87–8

ear piercing, 111
Eliot, Lisa, 27
Ellemers, Naomi, 16–17

Fatherhood Institute, 11
fathers, 138–43
Fawcett Society, 10–11, 142
Featherstone, Dr Brid, 141–2
female characters, as role models for boys and girls, 47
femininity, 112–13
value placed on, 48–9
feminism, 118–23
and awareness, 110–11
journey, xv–xvi

films
gender bias, 47–8, 58
racial diversity, 56
studies of, 53–4
Fine, Cordelia, 9, 106
Fisher, Fox and Owl, 161
Following Young Fathers, 141
food, designs on clothing, 85
freedom of choice, 20–1
Frozen (film), 47–8
Future Men, 138, 143

Geena Davis Institute on Gender in Media, 51–5, 59
gender, xiv
assigned to neutral characters in books, 33–4
and brain structure, 5
grammatical, 100–1
grouping study, 25
vs sex, xiii
vs sexual orientation, 14
as a spectrum, 147, 156
gender bias, 5–7, 176–7
in children's books, 32–8
on children's TV, 46
in films, 47–8, 58
Gender Development Laboratory, 69
gender dysphoria, 157
gender identity, 145
gender inequality, 118–23
gender stereotypes, 15–16, 173–7
addressing by parents, 10–11, 26, 28–9
awareness of, 167–73

effect on brain, 9–11
in clothing, 11, 82–91
expectations on young
   children, 14–15, 17, 171
freedom of choice, 20–1
growing up with, 112–18,
   133–8, 153–4
in language, 97, 100–8
perceptions of abilities,
   16–17, 70
problematic for boys, 103–6
in sports, 70
about STEM subjects, 17–19
of toys, 11, 24, 68–70
in TV shows, 50, 54–5
understanding level of very
   young children, 50
vicious cycle, 21, 70
genderfluid people, 158
genderqueer people, 158
Genderspectrum (website), 27,
   155
genitalia, awareness of, 150
Girl Guiding UK, 122–3
Girls on Film (podcast), 59
Good Night Stories of Rebel
   Girls, 123
Google, 120

Hebb, Donald, 4
HeForShe, 123
Hello Society Kids, 91–3
Hildreth, Cade, xiii
homosexuality, 148–50
   'worries' about in young
      children, 14
Hoyes, Melanie, 56–9

IamRemarkable, 120
*Importance of Representation
   in Film and Media, The*
   (Washington), 59
Indonesia, 159
innateness, as a 'starter pack', 5
inner voice, 103
intersex people, xiii–xiv, 155

job applications, 116–17
Johnson, Katharine et al, 105

Kuklin, Susan, 161

language
   gender differences in
      development, 99–100
   gender distinction in, 95–6
   gender-neutral, 107–8
   gender stereotypes, 97, 100–8
   grammatical gender, 100–1
   parent–child interaction,
      98–9, 105
   self-talk, 96–7
LeanIn, 120
Learning for Justice (website),
   27
learning process,
   neuroplasticity, 2–5, 8–9
Let Books Be Books, 72
Let Clothes Be Clothes, 90
Let Toys Be Toys, 11, 64–6, 71,
   72–5
LGBTQ+ community
   mental health, 154
   non-binary people, 145–6,
      147–8, 151–5, 157–63

trans binary people, 145–6, 156–7
Lifting Limits, 11
love, developing an understanding of, 150–1

Marshall, Jeffrey, 152
masculinity, 138–43
and awareness, 126–8
and mental health, 130
social norms, 130–2, 136–8
value placed on, 48–9, 135
Mask You Live In, The, 27
maternity leave, 175
mathematics, 19 (see also STEM subjects)
attitudes vs aptitudes, 19
media, 45–8, 56–9
studies of, 48–55
Mediasmarts (website), 27
Men Engage, 142
Men in the Early Years, 11
Men Who Hate Women (Bates), 135
menstrual cycle, biased research, 9
mental health, 130
gender dysphoria, 157
in the LGBTQ+ community, 154
meritocracy, 20, 21
Mermaids, 160–1
Mighty Girl, A (website), 27, 123
Mika & Lolo (Mendez), 31–2, 38
mindfulness, 3
Miss Representation, 27

nature vs nurture debate, 3–4, 5, 166
Neurogenderings, 9
neuroplasticity, 2–5, 8–9
'No more boys and girls' documentary, 7, 106
non-binary people, 145–6, 147–8, 151–5, 157–63 (see also trans binary people)

O'Mara, Peggy, 103
Open University, 142

Paoletti, Jo B., 83
parenting, xvi–xvii, 164–6
accidental gender bias, 5–6, 17, 22, 176–7
addressing gender stereotypes, 10–11, 26, 28–9
bringing up boys, 126, 143–4
bringing up girls, 120–2, 124–5
bringing up non-binary children, 160–1
decisions on toys, 74–7
leading by example, 110, 142, 172
stay-at-home parents, 20
teaching about consent, 128–9
verbal interaction with children, 98–9, 105
Paw Patrol (TV show), 46
personality
gender expectations, 14–15
value placed on masculine vs feminine traits, 48–9

Piaget, Jean, 18
'pinkification'
  of clothing, 82–3
  of toys, 67–8
podcasts, 59
Poundland, 83
Power Pose, 120
Promundo, 54–5, 130–1
pronouns, in children's books, 106

Queer project, 158

racial diversity, 38
  in films, 56
resources, 27, 42, 122–3, 142–3, 177
  on language use, 106
  on media, 59
  on non-binary children, 160–1, 163
  for toys, 75
Rippon, Gina, 5, 8–11
role models
  in books, 36–7
  female characters as role models for boys and girls, 47
  at home, 172
Roomes, Emma, 84

Saini, Angela, 104–5, 106
Sammaritano, Francesca, 86
Sandberg, Sheryl, 120
Sanders, Jayneen and Jess, 39–42
schools, 113–14
  gender stereotypes in, 11
  gender stereotypes in language, 106
  grouping by gender, 25
  STEM subjects, 17–19
self-esteem, 122–3
self-talk, 96–7
sex (biological)
  and brain structure, 4
  explaining to children, 13–14
  finding out during pregnancy, 174
  vs gender, xiii
  intersex people, xiii–xiv, 155
  as a spectrum, 147
sexual activity, teaching about, 132–3
sexual assault, victims of, 132
sexual orientation, 148–50, 158
  vs gender, 14
  'worries' about in young children, 14
sexualization, 150
  of boys, 131–2
  of clothing, 86–7, 89
  of older girls, 114–15
  of younger girls, 113
Shaw, Leanne, 65–6
Shinta Ratri, 159
shoes, 89–90
shopping, segregation of toys, 71
slogans on clothing, 83–4
Smith, Anna, 59
'Smurfette principle', 46
socioeconomic status, and brain structure, 3
Sonshine Magazine, 103–6
Spanish, grammatical gender, 101

Spears Brown, Christia, 23–4, 95
sports
  gender stereotypes in
    language, 103
  perceptions of abilities, 70
stay-at-home parents, 20
STEM subjects, 17–19
stereotypes, 15 (see also gender
  stereotypes)
Stryker, Susan, 161
Sweet, Dr Elizabeth, 73–4
synaptic plasticity, 4

teachers, gender bias in books,
  36–7
Think or Blue, 173, 174
Thomas, Owen, 138–43
toys, 74–7
  campaigns about, 72–5
  colour coded, 67–8
  gender stereotypes, 11, 24,
    68–70
  as learning tools, 63–6
  segregation in shops, 71

twentieth-century marketing,
  73–4
Trabue, Tessa, 72–5
trans binary people, 145–6,
  156–7 (see also non-binary
  people)
transitioning, 157
TV shows, 45
  choosing, 60–2
  studies of, 48–52, 54–5

Ubuntu, 142
unconscious bias, 5–6, 16–17, 22

Wamsley, Laurel, 155
Waria people, 159
Washington, Lauren, 59
websites, 27
Williams, Georgie, 155, 158–61
Wilson, Hannah, 118–23
#WomenEd, 118, 119–20

YouTube videos, 27
Yu-Moran, Janice, 91–3

Acknowledgements

This book couldn't exist without Chris, who has corrected, edited, made suggestions and encouraged me every step of the way. Parenting is much more fun with you. Everything is much more fun with you.

And obviously without Eric and Nora. I hope by the time you are old enough to read the book you do it with pride, and you feel the unconditional love and honest admiration that I have for you both. You teach me so much every day.

To my brilliant mentor and friend Emer, the first person that I send all book related updates to. You have helped me so much in the last years, you have made me overcome the fear of querying, held my hand when drafting the proposal and celebrated with me every single step until publication day. I am so grateful for you.

To my sister Irene, the childfree surgeon, cool auntie and counter-stereotypical role model with rainbow hair that my kids are going to want to impress. I don't blame them, you are pretty awesome.

To my fantastic editor Victoria Roddam, you have always made me feel able to do this. You have polished the book, making it better, encouraged me and believed in my project. Thank you.

To Becky Thomas, it is very cool having an agent at all, but it is even cooler having YOU as an agent.

To everyone that is interviewed, to Nic and Cat. You add so much value and your expertise is invaluable, I am so humbled and excited about sharing it!

To Rosie, Filomena, Hannah, Maja and Lauren for your help with the research, the querying and your honest opinions and feedback. I know you were supposed to be learning from me in your internships, but I have learnt a lot from you too. I am so excited about your generation.

To Grace for keeping me right when speaking about neuro-plasticity, and for sacrificing your computer when reading my book with red wine on a Friday night. Ooops.

To Clare Willets, it is so great to have someone pre-reading your book who just gets it, who knows exactly why.

To Astra, for bringing value and reminding me that it is ok to be emotional, that emotional is powerful.

To Jo-Ann Finkelstein. For reading the book and making the most relevant points and observations, you are one of the smartest people I know! Thanks for your genuine, honest happiness about this book happening. I can't wait to read yours.

To Jane Anderson, Cara Bolton, Eva Nieto and Marcus McComb for being my accountability partners and coming back with reassuring feedback and good ideas.

To Nikki. I only asked you to review it at the very end because I know that your unreal level of attention to detail would have been wasted in all the other versions, and even if I had told you just to read it diagonally you couldn't have stopped yourself.

To Lisa and my coaching gang and our way to learn about saboteurs' voices.

To Franchine and our weekly walks that kept me sane.

To Almu, it doesn't matter how life or distance try to get in the way, you are always there.

To everyone that sent me a message to check in on the book, that smiled behind the screen or in real life with the updates and felt part of it. You are. Unsurprisingly writing a book ended up being quite an emotional thing and you always made me feel that I had a whole village supporting me. Now make sure you buy the book and recommend it!

To all the children in the world, I am genuinely excited about what you are going to do next and how you are going to transform this society into something better. I know you will.

About the Author

Virginia Mendez is a mother of two and the co-founder of www.thefeministshop.com. She is the author of two books for children on gender, and consent. As a children's author, she has spoken to over 2000 school children, promoting critical thinking and inviting them to understand what is behind their already-formed ideas about things being for boys and things being for girls. She has spoken at the Human Rights Festival, has been featured in both *Forbes* and *The Belfast Telegraph*, and is part of the thought leader program 'Ladies who Launch'. She has been featured in Women in Business and she is frequently invited to podcasts and YouTube channels as a guest speaker. Virginia is part of the Global Equality Collective, and DiverseEducators. She has been recognised as one of the 145 Inspiring Women Leaders of 2020 by Diverse In Globaland and won an award as one of the Top 100 UK #iAlso f:Entrepreneurs in 2020.

Notes